The story of

BOB MARLEY

WELCOME

In recent years, the word 'legend' has become increasingly overused and clichéd, whether used to describe a mildly successful sports star or fleetingly popular musician. However, in reality, there are few individuals truly deserving of the praise. One man who the word represents better than almost any other, however, is Bob Marley – a true musical great and, indeed, a bona fide legend.

Forty years after he was cruelly cut down in his prime, we celebrate Bob Marley's life, music and legacy and tell the incredible story of his rise from the Kingston ghetto to become an international superstar. We explore his faith and spirituality, as well as his revolutionary message, and discover how they shaped the man and his music and won over legions of fans from across the globe.

Filled with iconic imagery and fascinating insight, we also delve into Marley's best loved albums with track-by-track breakdowns of the likes of the ground-breaking *Catch a Fire* and the mighty *Exodus*. So sit back, crank up the volume and enjoy the story of the legend himself, Bob Marley.

Credit: Getty Images

The story of

BOB MARLEY

Future PLC Quay House, The Ambury, Bath, BA1 1UA

Editorial
Editor **Dan Peel**
Senior Designer **Phil Martin**
Senior Art Editor **Andy Downes**
Head of Art & Design **Greg Whitaker**
Editorial Director **Jon White**

Contributors
Edoardo Albert, Hareth Al Bustani, Josephine Hall, Adam Quarshie

Cover images
AF archive / Alamy Stock Photo

Photography
All copyrights and trademarks are recognised and respected

Advertising
Media packs are available on request
Commercial Director **Clare Dove**

International
Head of Print Licensing **Rachel Shaw**
licensing@futurenet.com
www.futurecontenthub.com

Circulation
Head of Newstrade **Tim Mathers**

Production
Head of Production **Mark Constance**
Production Project Manager **Matthew Eglinton**
Advertising Production Manager **Joanne Crosby**
Digital Editions Controller **Jason Hudson**
Production Managers **Keely Miller, Nola Cokely,
Vivienne Calvert, Fran Twentyman**

Printed by William Gibbons, 26 Planetary Road,
Willenhall, West Midlands, WV13 3XT

Distributed by Marketforce, 5 Churchill Place, Canary Wharf, London, E14 5HU
www.marketforce.co.uk Tel: 0203 787 9001

The Story of Bob Marley First Edition (MUB3892)
© 2021 Future Publishing Limited

Future plc is a public
company quoted on the
London Stock Exchange
(symbol: FUTR)
www.futureplc.com

Chief executive **Zillah Byng-Thorne**
Non-executive chairman **Richard Huntingford**
Chief financial officer **Rachel Addison**

Tel +44 (0)1225 442 244

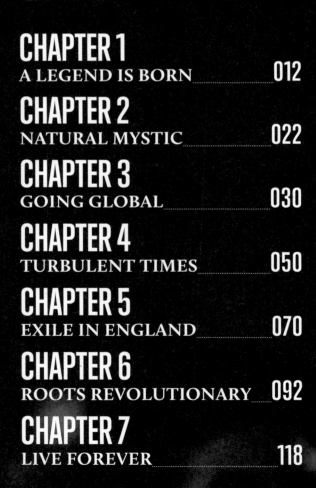

CONTENTS

![brushstroke]

FOREWORD

Legendary DJ and filmmaker Don Letts on meeting Bob Marley, what his music means to millions and why he'll continue to live on

I was born in the UK – first generation British-born Black. Easy to say now but back then it was a confusing concept – trust me. Growing up against a backdrop of racial tension, our only solace came in the form of music. In those days it was the emerging sounds of Jamaica that helped us find our feet. By the early 1970s this had morphed from the good times sounds of ska and rocksteady into something more militant and more politicised. The group that typified that change was The Wailers with the release of 1973's *Catch a Fire*. Now don't get it twisted, Bob, Peter [Tosh] and Bunny [Wailer] had already established themselves in that arena and appeared on the UK reggae radar long before, having released close to a hundred singles up to that point. Indeed, tracks like 'Duppy Conqueror' and 'Who is Mr Brown' had already captured the imagination of this child of Windrush, not to mention albums like 1970's *Soul Rebels* (produced by Lee 'Scratch' Perry).

ABOVE LEFT *Marley's music had a profound effect on Black youth growing up in Britain and elsewhere in the 1970s.*

LEFT *Don befriended Marley after sneaking into his hotel after The Wailers' Lyceum Theatre gig in 1975.*

But it was the release of *Catch a Fire* that set Bob on his meteoric rise. When Island Records' boss Chris Blackwell first met him, he thought Bob was the 'living embodiment' of the rebel outlaw and street poet portrayed by Jimmy Cliff's character in the film *The Harder They Come*. Driven by his belief in the band's potential, Blackwell pulled out all the stops for the album's production and packaging. Up till then most album artwork looked like badly printed postcards, but *Catch a Fire* came in a gated sleeve imitating a Zippo lighter, giving it parity with the rock albums of the day. To enhance what was a lyrically and sonically complex creation Chris Blackwell brought in Wayne Perkins and John 'Rabbit' Bundrick to provide some overdubs. They put some touches to the songs that maybe Bob Marley and the Wailers would not have done, but Bob was nobody's fool. If he had not wanted them on the record they would not have been on it. Tracks like 'Concrete Jungle' referred to the state of urban poverty and 'Slave Driver' connected past injustices to the present times. Interestingly, the lyrical content and subject matter translated perfectly to the eager ears of the lost UK tribes on the streets of London and as such the record was a revelation.

When Bob Marley came along he was not just playing music, he embodied the Rasta ideology.

> # THE LEGENDARY LYCEUM GIG WAS THE SINGLE MOST EXCITING MUSIC MOMENT OF MY LIFE.

For a young Black kid growing up in Babylon the message was radical and inspiring. Later that same year, The Wailers released *Burnin'*. Opening with 'Get Up, Stand Up', it was a call to action that took the militant themes on *Catch a Fire* to another level. It would also be Bob's last album with Peter Tosh and Bunny Wailer. 1974's *Natty Dread* was also important to me. It too reflected on the political turmoil swallowing up Jamaica with songs like '3 O'Clock Roadblock' and 'Them Belly Full (But We Hungry)'. But tracks like 'No Woman, No Cry' revealed Bob as a double-edged sword. On one side the rude boy rebel, on the other consciousness and love.

The following year I went to Bob Marley's legendary gig at the Lyceum. It was the single most exciting music moment of my life and the closest I've ever been to a 'religious' experience. He came on, dropped 'Trenchtown Rock' and the crowd went wild. The note-perfect Wailers, now supplemented by the I Threes, played a faultless set and Bob's performance was inspired. He seemed to be infected with the same sense of optimistic enthusiasm as everyone in the crowd. As the music flowed and the singing grew in volume (you almost couldn't hear Bob during 'Get Up, Stand Up', the call and response was deafening), it seemed as if life was going to be alright, that everyone in that room was ready,

MECCA **LYCEUM** The Strand, London WC2

A.L.E. Limited in association with Island Artists

present

BOB MARLEY and the WAILERS

and Special Guests

THIRD WORLD

on FRIDAY 18th JULY 1975 at 7.30 p.m.

Tickets £1.50

ABOVE *A ticket to the legendary Lyceum show, which Don describes as being close to a 'religious experience'.*

OPPOSITE *Don was heavily involved in the punk scene in the 1970s and went on to work with the likes of The Clash.*

willing and able to go out and make everything better no matter what it took. It wasn't spoken out loud and I didn't have that exact thought at the time, but I felt that something was happening, that here was a man who could teach me something important about the world. We'd been thrashing around with this British Black/Black British identity crisis and then the full impact and reality of what we had heard on his records came together in that show. It was no longer an abstract thing that you could interpret one way or another. Here was the man on stage delivering it live and direct, and giving me confidence to be me.

After the gig I followed Bob Marley in my car back to his hotel in Harrington Gardens in South Kensington. Like someone possessed, I marched into the hotel with all the other Rasta brethren. Everyone was sitting down and I found a little spot in the corner. Bob was holding court in his room, smoking herb and reasoning with all the UK Rastas. Finally, it was three or four in the morning and Bob had out-reasoned and out-smoked everybody. He looked around the room and saw me with my baby dreads and tiny but fortunately potent bag of weed. I was called to the table whereupon Bob proceeded to smoke off my herb, by which time I'd managed to make my presence felt.

A few days later I went back to get a picture of Bob with myself before he returned to Jamaica. I had a Polaroid camera and the band and Bob were like, "bloodclaat instant picture". Polaroid technology had not yet reached Jamaica so everybody wanted a picture with Bob. Ten pictures down, I still hadn't got my picture of me and Bob. So I ran to a local

store to purchase some more Polaroid film. By the time I got back Bob's chef and his crew had turned up and decided they also wanted a picture. After one more trip to the store I finally got mine.

In 1977, Bob returned to London staying in Oakley Street off the King's Road, Chelsea. He was effectively in exile after he had been shot in Jamaica. It was an attempt to prevent him from performing at the Smile Jamaica concert, which was aimed at uniting the two warring political parties. This was during the birth of the UK punk rock movement during which time I was running a store called Acme Attractions on the Kings Road and Bob's chosen location gave him a front row seat to the emerging scene. I went round to his house one time to collect money for some weed wearing my punk-style bondage trousers. On seeing them he exclaimed, "What ya deal wid Don Letts, dem nasty punk rockers, yu look like a bloodclaat mountaineer!" To which I replied, "Bredrin', dem crazy baldheads are my friends, we're like-minded rebels." Bob kissed his teeth and basically told me to take a hike. But during his UK stay he became more familiar with the real deal (as opposed to the tabloid version) and was moved to record 'Punky Reggae Party'.

Between 1976 and his final album – 1983's *Confrontation* – Bob released five more studio albums, all of which helped to shape me in so many ways. Indeed it was the confidence and self-belief he instilled in me, along with some punk attitude, that helped me to become a filmmaker. A few years after Bob's passing I had the honour of directing the 'One Love' and 'Waiting in Vain' videos along with the long-form video for 'Legend'. So it's fair to say I wouldn't be the man I am today if it wasn't for Bob. He's left an outstanding body of work that will continue to do for others what it did for me.

In the 21st century Bob Marley remains the most globally recognised artist on Earth and that's not just down to sales – far from it. Truth be told as long as there is inequality on the planet, Bob will remain the voice of the people.

DON LETTS
The Rebel Dread

***There and Black Again: Don Letts: The Autobiography** is out now on Omnibus Press.*

CHAPTER ONE

A LEGEND
IS BORN

A LEGEND IS BORN

Abandoned and rejected from childhood, Bob Marley's journey from village palm reader to Trench Town Rasta rocker was driven by a sense of destiny

WORDS BY **HARETH AL BUSTANI**

In 1944, Cedella Malcolm, an 18-year-old Black Jamaican woman, found out she was pregnant and immediately married her lover, the older White British plantation overseer, Captain Norval Marley. Norval's racist family disapproved of the union, and despite being around 60 years old, he succumbed to their pressure, abandoning his pregnant wife. Cedella gave birth to their son on 6 February 1945, in the sleepy village of Nine Mile, in the hills of north Jamaica's Saint Ann Parish. Norval returned briefly to meet his son and helped decide on a name – Nesta Robert 'Bob' Marley – but, with that settled, he was gone.

Cedella's own father, Omariah, a local medicine man, played a formative role in baby Bob's upbringing, teaching him "not to steal" and to "tell the truth". Bob helped tend to Omariah's lands; moving animals around, cutting and gathering corn and fetching spring water. From the age of three, he had become somewhat of a local phenomenon for his ability to read peoples' palms with remarkable accuracy. Although Nine Mile had no electricity or running water, every Sunday Omariah would plug in his generator, tune his radio into a Miami station and play music for the locals. Listening to the latest hits from Elvis Presley and Fats Domino with his cousin was one of Bob's highlights of the week.

When Bob was five years old, his biological father showed up and asked Cedella to send him to Jamaica's capital, Kingston, so he could get a proper education. Reluctantly, she agreed. However, as soon as they arrived in the city, Norval sent his son to live with an elderly friend. Cedella wrote to her husband, asking if she could visit, only to be told not to bother – their son was enlisted in a boarding school in Saint Thomas. In reality, he was left to his own devices, roaming the capital's rough streets, often spending weeks without a decent meal. Two years later, when someone from Nine Mile recognised Bob on the street, his mother promptly brought him back to the village. When he returned, people anxiously asked him to read their palms, only to be told, "No, I'm not reading no more hand, I'm singing now".

In 1957, Bob befriended nine-year-old Neville 'Bunny' Livingston (later known as Bunny Wailer), who had just moved to Nine Mile. Bunny recalled Bob was a bit of a "wild child". "He was like the ugly duckling," he said. "Nobody wanted him around their corn, so he get what's left. He just had to survive." As a mixed-race boy, Bob was rejected by both sides of his family on racial grounds. To some, his fair skin was a physical representation of

OPPOSITE *(Left to right) Bunny Wailer, Bob Marley and Peter Tosh as The Wailers in 1964.*

CHAPTER ONE

centuries of brutal British colonial rule and slavery. This rejection drove Bob to develop strength of will, independence and introspection.

TRENCH TOWN ROCK

When Bob was ten, he learned that his father had died. Soon after, he and his mother relocated to Kingston again, moving in with Bunny and his father, Toddy. Cedella and Toddy had a daughter together, making Bob and Bunny brothers of sorts. They lived in an area at the edge of the port called Trench Town, an overcrowded concrete jungle, filled with Soviet-style, low-income 'government yards' – built to give poor people housing and running water. Unemployment was rife, and because no employer wanted to hire anyone living in the ghetto, the only ways out were through music or sport. One could scarcely turn a corner without hearing aspiring young vocal groups crooning through the latest hits.

Jamaica was in the grip of the exciting offbeat rhythms and walking basslines of ska – a brand-new sound, blending American jazz and rhythm and blues with Caribbean mento and calypso. One of the first new friends Bob made was the singer Segree

Wesley. Bob, Bunny and Segree would practise singing together in the kitchen.

Bob also lived just a stone's throw from one of Jamaica's earliest recording artists, Joe Higgs, who recalled: "Bob was known as a very light-skinned chap living in the ghetto. People called him the little red boy, and he would be beaten up by a lot of guys." At the request of a mutual friend, Joe started giving Bob singing lessons: "We would meet early in the mornings, and whatever I did, soccer, go to the sea, he would be among us. I was always giving him insight into the music."

Toddy did not provide for Bob, so – at Cedella's insistence – he went to learn welding. Still suffering from neglect, Bob quickly developed a reputation as a local 'rude boy', and his street-fighting skills earned him the nickname 'Tuff Gong'. However, Bob worked hardest on his musical abilities, rehearsing with Bunny, another young singer Junior Braithwaite, and a few local talents. One day, while working as a welder, Bob was injured when a stray spark hit his eye. With that, he quit the trade and became more determined than ever to make a career in music.

Through one of his welding colleagues, the successful rocksteady singer, Desmond Dekker, Bob

Credit: Getty Images

ABOVE *Desmond Dekker, who had a hit in 1968 with 'Israelites' helped Bob catch his big break.*

LEFT *An early image of Bob and the band.*

RIGHT *After making waves in Jamaica, Bob Marley and the Wailers signed with Island Records in 1972.*

was introduced to the legendary Chinese-Jamaican record producer Leslie Kong, who owned the iconic Beverley's record label. Dekker took Bob into the studio with him, and once he'd finished recording his own track, 'Honour Your Mother and Father', the 17-year-old Bob went in and recorded four songs, including a track he had written himself, 'Judge Not'.

With his first original track, Bob signalled a desire to write songs that bore weight, singing: "I know that I'm not perfect, and that I don't claim to be, so before you point your fingers, be sure your hands are clean". Another song he recorded, 'One Cup of Coffee', was released under the pseudonym Bobby Martell. Although the recordings hardly catapulted Bob to fame, he walked out of the session with £20, which went towards some new clothes. Soon after, he met a kindred spirit called Winston Hubert McIntosh – better known as Peter Tosh.

SIMMER DOWN

Peter was abandoned by his parents as a boy and had largely grown up raising himself. He was a remarkably talented musician, who'd taught himself to play the organ, guitar and percussion. He and Bob immediately hit it off. Peter taught the group to harmonise, and showed Bob how to play the guitar. Together with Bunny, the trio formed a vocal group, called The Wailing Wailers. To expand their sound, they began rehearsing with Braithwaite and two female singers, Beverley Kelso and Cherry Smith.

The band's name was a nod to the suffering that characterised not just their own upbringings, but the zeitgeist of a Jamaica that had only just achieved independence from Britain. Author Roger Steffens explained, "To wail, in Jamaican terms, meant to cry out for justice, to beseech the Almighty, and the powers that be for a better life". In 1964, Kingston was consumed by unemployment, crime, overcrowding and misery. The Wailers wanted to write songs that did not simply distract people from their problems, but brought them to the forefront of the national consciousness.

Joe Higgs continued to train the group, who approached Leslie Kong's rival, Studio One, owned

BOB MARLEY

EARL LINDO

PETER TOSH

JOE HIGGS

ASTON "FAMILY MAN" BARRETT

CARLTON BARRETT

THE WAILERS

island records
available from capitol reco

Credit: Getty Images

"
I DON'T COME TO BOW, I COME TO CONQUER.

– BOB MARLEY

by producer Clement 'Coxsone' Dodd – one of Jamaica's most powerful music moguls. Coxsone sent the band in to record one of Bob's songs 'Simmer Down', backed by The Skatalites – a supergroup that had pioneered and popularised the ska genre. With crime rates soaring, and the increasingly factional political process beginning to incorporate gang and drug lords, 'Simmer Down' was directed at Kingston's 'rude boys', telling them to calm down in language they would understand.

The song was a phenomenon, soaring to the top of the Jamaican charts, and selling 80,000 records – at a time where 5,000 was considered a hit. Radio stations blasting throughout the day, over and over, and Jamaica's insatiable demand for the song kept four record pressing plants busy round the clock.

The group would huddle around a campfire and listen as Bob plucked out some new songs on his guitar, working the tunes out under the stars. In the studio, they rotated on vocals – Braithwaite sang lead on his Curtis Mayfield-inspired ballad 'It Hurts To Be Alone' in a stunning Frankie Lymon-esque voice, just days before leaving for the United States. However, while everyone had their own strengths, Bob was emerging as the natural leader.

Over the next year, The Wailers churned out a steady stream of original hits, punctuated by covers like The Beatles' 'And I Love Her'. Solid musicianship provided a forgiving anchor of professionalism, against which Bob could hone his own vocal talents. A veteran of the 1950s' mobile disco 'sound system' craze, Coxsone began booking public performances, and the band rapidly developed their stage presence. Bunny remembered a gig at Kingston's Palace Theatre, where The Wailers were doing the splits and leaping over each other: "The people never seen nothing like that in Jamaica before". At one point, when the power cut out, a group of thugs started tearing the place apart, an incident that inspired The Wailers to later record potentially the first true 'rude boy' song, 'Hooligan'.

By 1965, The Wailers simultaneously had the number one, two, three, five and seven songs in the charts. Yet, even after releasing a commercially successful compilation album, they were yet to reap any of the financial rewards.

DUPPY CONQUEROR

In 1966, Bob went to visit his mother in the United States for nine months. Before leaving, he married his girlfriend, Rita Anderson, a single mother and singer. While he was gone, Jamaica was graced by a momentous visit of the Ethiopian Emperor Haile Selassie – who was seen as a messiah by Jamaica's growing Rastafari religious movement. Just days

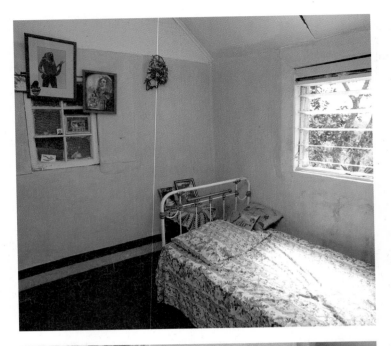

Credit: Alamy

OPPOSITE, RIGHT *The legendary Lee 'Scratch' Perry produced two of Bob Marley and the Wailers' early albums.*

OPPOSITE, TOP LEFT *Peter Tosh was a self-taught guitarist and the only member of the band who could play instruments initially.*

OPPOSITE, BOTTOM LEFT *Bunny Wailer, a childhood friend of Bob's and one of The Wailers' original members.*

TOP *A single bed in the bedroom of Bob's childhood home in Nine Mile.*

ABOVE *Memorabilia and images of Bob on the walls of his childhood home, which is now a museum.*

after Selassie left the island, Peter Tosh recorded a track called 'Rasta Shook Them Up'. When Bob returned, the country was electric with excitement. So was he. Hoping to finally break free from the exploitative nature of the music industry, he used the $700 he raised working odd jobs in the US to start an ill-fated record label, Wail 'n Soul'm.

Around the same time, he also met Mortimo Planno, a Rasta high priest, who became his spiritual advisor and introduced him to the successful American singer-songwriter, Johnny Nash. Bob increasingly devoted himself to Rastafarianism, smoking copious amounts of marijuana and growing his hair into dreadlocks. He took a break from recording and retreated with Rita to his grandfather's farm in Nine Mile (Omariah had passed away in 1965). While there, Bob took time to meditate on The Wailers' future.

When the band returned to Kingston in late 1968, they had a new attitude, new music, and a new mission. After a misguided stint at Johnny Nash's JAD Records, they worked briefly with Leslie Kong again, before finally striking up a relationship with the furiously innovative Lee 'Scratch' Perry. Suddenly, their songs were infused with Rasta lyrics

and drumming – making them arguably the first popular Jamaican group to do so. By now, Bob had honed his voice, developing a hypnotic otherworldly delivery, perfectly suited to its spiritually charged material. The band's lyrics became increasingly socially conscious, reflecting issues of colonialism and Pan-Africanism.

Their music showed a transition from ska to rocksteady, slowing down to rhythmic grooves, and brass pulled out to make way for guitar breakdowns. This new philosophy resulted in the 1970 album, *Soul Rebels*, which featured stripped back musical arrangements, a pioneering entry into the emerging reggae genre. They followed this musical evolution with a spiritual revolution, with newer compositions, declaring, "I've got to reach Mount Zion", and "Got to have Kaya [marijuana] now".

The follow-up to *Soul Rebels*, *Soul Revolution*, was such a commercial hit, it landed The Wailers a tour of Britain. At the end of the tour, they were offered a contract by Island Records – The Wailers were going international. Just before his death in 1971 Leslie Kong released a compilation of new material called *The Best of The Wailers*. But, for Bob, the best was yet to come.

CHAPTER TWO

NATURAL MYSTIC

NATURAL MYSTIC

Bob Marley lived his faith more than any other music star but there was more to that faith than the green, red and gold of Rastafarianism

WORDS BY **EDOARDO ALBERT**

Bob Marley was no ordinary pop star. At the heart of what set him apart from the usual production line of musical celebrities was faith: Marley lived, embodied and preached his faith more openly, and more successfully, than any revivalist preacher or television evangelist. Religion – and it was religion, not some sort of cafeteria spirituality – was at the very centre of his being. But as to the exact nature of the religion that Marley followed, that is a little harder to ascertain. This might seem strange as Marley is everywhere associated, in colours of red, green and gold, with Rastafarianism, the dreadlocked prophet of the new faith that had sprung up in Jamaica in the 1930s. But the story of Bob Marley's religious faith, and where it took him, is more convoluted than it seems.

While Marley came to be associated with Kingston's tough Trench Town district, his roots and his early life were in the countryside, in the idyllic environs of Nine Mile in Saint Ann Parish in the north of Jamaica. The community in which Marley grew up had no doubt that this world is a battlefield in which spiritual forces – some benign, others malignant – contend. It was a world in which a Bible-steeped Christianity mixed and merged with traditional African animist beliefs expressed in Obeah producing a world that existed on the border between the material and the spiritual. Dreams,

visions, voices and possessions were all part of this; throughout his life Marley had vivid dreams and a calm acceptance of the stream-of-consciousness speech of people that, in the West, would be labelled as mentally ill. As a boy, Bob read palms, seeing people's future in the lines on their hands.

The Bible lay at the centre of Marley's life and its cadences, rhythms and phrases fill his songs. He carried his well-thumbed copy of the venerable King James translation everywhere he went, and Marley did more than most people to bring its poetry back into the consciousness of today, even if many of his listeners did not recognise the quotations and allusions peppering his work. Indeed, Marley's very first release, 'Judge Not', is a reference to Jesus's injunction, "Judge not, lest ye be judged."

It was from this Bible-steeped milieu that the faith with which Marley was to be most closely associated grew. Rastafari developed in Jamaica from the 1930s, its growth fuelled by the crowning of Haile Selassie as Emperor of Ethiopia in 1930. Street preachers interpreted Selassie's coronation as the fulfilment of Biblical prophecies, and the movement took its name from Ras Tafari, Selassie's title and first name. Its deeper roots lie in the Black consciousness movement founded by Jamaican-born Marcus Garvey and in particular Garvey's direction, "Look to Africa, when a Black king shall be crowned, for the day of deliverance is at hand."

Among the most influential of these early preachers was Leonard Howell who, upon returning to Jamaica after travels abroad, established a community called Pinnacle in the mountainous area of Saint Catherine where he started growing marijuana as a cash crop. Soon, marijuana smoking became a distinctive part of Rastafarian practice, the ritual partaking of the herb believed to draw the believer into closer communion with Jah. Unfortunately, it also provoked clashes with the authorities as marijuana was illegal. After a number of raids, Pinnacle was disbanded by the police in the 1950s. However, by that time Rastafarians had spread throughout the island, some living in Kingston where the faith began to make inroads among the poor and musicians.

Marley first encountered its teachings in a serious way during his days at Studio One. Some of the musicians there were devout Rastafarians and they would expound on passages in Marley's Bible in ways that seemed to bring the wider world and his own experience of it into sharp focus. There was a

Credit: Getty Images

RASTAFARI NOT A CULTURE, IT'S A REALITY.

– BOB MARLEY ON RASTAFARIANISM

strongly apocalyptic and millenarian strand to this new faith that appealed to the young Marley.

However, Marley was still not sure about his place in this new religion. This would change in 1966 when one of the most important events in the history of Rastafarianism occurred: Emperor Haile Selassie, the Lion of Judah himself, arrived in the country. Only, Marley missed it – he was in America, visiting his mother at the time. But his wife, Rita Marley, had stayed in Jamaica, so he wrote to her asking that she go and see this man whom the Rastafarians proclaimed to be a living god.

On 21 April 1966, Rita, along with 100,000 Rastafarians and curious onlookers, descended on the airport and the route into the capital. Rita waited on the route but, at the airport, all crowd control broke down and it required a Rastafarian elder, Mortimo Planno, to convince the crowd to step back and allow the Emperor off the plane. Waiting in the rain amid a crush of people, Rita saw the Daimler bringing Haile Selassie into Kingston approaching. Rita had also been thinking of converting to Rastafarianism, and was looking for a sign to confirm or deny that inclination. Then, as the limousine passed, Haile Selassie looked into the crowd, into Rita's eyes, smiled and waved. On his raised hand, Rita saw the print of a nail: the

stigmata. The vision confirmed her belief that Haile Selassie was indeed Christ himself, reborn on Earth to usher in the millennium. The anniversary of Haile Selassie's visit to Jamaica continues to be celebrated as a holy day by Rastafarians around the world, known as Grounation Day.

When Bob Marley returned to Jamaica, he was 21 years old and about to make a transformative change, a change manifested on the outside by beginning to grow out his hair. Marley sought out the man who had guided the Emperor himself down the steps from his plane, Mortimo Planno, and asked him for instruction in the teachings of Rastafari. Planno taught Marley the symbolism underlying the Rastafarian view of the world. Marley's fellow Wailers, Peter Tosh and Bunny Wailer, were also growing out their hair as the three men embraced the new faith.

Realising the potential within the young Marley, Planno extended his mentoring from the spiritual to the business, becoming Bob's unofficial manager. This, though, brought temptations to Planno, temptations he found difficult to overcome. So while Marley and The Wailers pestered him with questions of deep spiritual import while sharing ganja, the elder inveigled the group of earnest young men to include him at nightclub dances and parties.

While his teacher was proving to have a pick-and-mix attitude to Rastafarian codes for living, Marley was adopting them wholeheartedly. The lyrics of his songs show how the approach of Rastafarians to language had permeated his thoughts. Seeing English as the language of Babylon (Western capitalist society), Rastafarians developed Iyaric, a dialect that avoided some sounds and words, and changed others. For example, 'understand' became 'overstand' and 'hello' (which contains the sounds 'hell' and 'low', words with negative connotations) is avoided. 'I and I', a characteristic lyric in Marley's work, replaces 'we', and indicates the unity of the individual with Jah. 'Jah' itself is a shortened form of 'Jahweh'/'Yahweh', the Hebrew name of God.

Marley also adopted the Rastafarian Ital diet, which emphasises eating natural foods and has a strict injunction against pork. Once Marley became a star, a feature of his touring party was the way they would take over the floor of the hotel in which they were staying, setting up cooking pots and producing Ital food for the band. Another feature of the band's tours were their impassioned reasoning sessions in the tour bus, when Bibles would be produced and passages pointed out in support of a theological point. 'Reasoning' in Rastafarianism is theological argument and discussion using proof texts from the Bible and it was a key point of entry for Marley into the faith.

Meanwhile, in Ethiopia, things were stirring, for good and ill. First, the Emperor sent a bishop of the Ethiopian Orthodox Church to Jamaica to minister to the Rastafarians. The Ethiopian Orthodox Church is one of the oldest Christian churches in the world, with roots stretching back at least to the 4th century CE, and quite possibly to the 1st century. It is rigorously orthodox with a highly developed theology and, because it was an isolated island in a sea of Muslim kingdoms, it developed almost entirely independently of Christianity in Europe. If Rastafarians were looking for a Black church untouched by Babylon, this was it. So when Bishop Abuna Yesehaq arrived in Jamaica, he found many Rastafarians interested in his teachings. The sticking point for many, though, was the Emperor himself; to the bishop and his church, Haile Selassie was a man, to Rastafarians he was God.

However, Rastafarian belief in imperial divinity was put severely to the test in 1975. Amid famine and unrest in Ethiopia, a cabal of military officers seized power in 1974 and imprisoned the Emperor. In late August the following year, the new regime announced that Selassie had died from complications following an operation. In truth, he had been murdered. The regime that took power in Ethiopia proved to be one of the most brutal in post-colonial African history but, for Rastafarians, the more immediate dilemma was theological: how could their living God die? Some denied it. Others symbolised it. Bob Marley wrote 'Jah Live'. The song proclaimed that God could not be killed.

The question remained though: was the core belief of Rastafarianism – the divinity of the Emperor Haile Selassie – true? While Rita Marley and her children had been baptised into the Ethiopian Orthodox Church in 1972, Bob was the most visible, the most famous face of Rastafarianism in the world. Even so, Marley became friendly with Bishop Abuna Yesehaq and attended services at the Ethiopian Orthodox Church in New York. But on 21 September 1980, Marley collapsed while running in Central Park. The cancer that had been diagnosed in his big toe had spread throughout his body, to his lungs, liver and brain. He was dying.

Six weeks later, Marley was baptised into the Ethiopian Orthodox Church by Archbishop Abuna Yesehaq, taking the baptismal name Berhane Selassie. Marley died on 11 May the following year, his funeral rites being conducted by the Archbishop. So the man most fully identified with Rastafarianism died and was buried as a member of the Ethiopian Orthodox Church. For Marley, whose deepest wish had been to escape Babylon and find God, it was perhaps a fitting conclusion to his life that he should end it as a member of this proudly independent and ancient church.

Credit: Getty Images

LEFT *Emperor Haile Selassie meets members of the Rastafarian faith during his visit to Jamaica.*

RIGHT *Smoking marijuana was thought to draw the believer into closer communion with Jah.*

CHAPTER THREE

GOING GLOBAL

GOING GLOBAL

There had never been a Third World superstar before. By the end of 1973, Bob Marley was on the verge of being the face and sound of the developing world

WORDS BY **EDOARDO ALBERT**

In 1958, a rich young man, out sailing his boat near Hellshire Beach, southwest of Kingston, ran onto the offshore reef. Unable to float the boat off, he swam to shore to seek assistance but found the beach deserted. Looking for help, dehydrated and parched, the young man collapsed, only to be rescued and nursed back to health by some fishermen. The rich young man was Chris Blackwell, scion on his father's side of the Crosse & Blackwell brand and on his mother's side of one of the richest families in Jamaica. As for the fishermen, they were Rastafarians. So when Blackwell started up Island Records in 1959, he was well disposed to an element of Jamaican society that was generally despised by the island elite. Moving to Britain in 1962, Blackwell took with him the rights he had acquired to Jamaican sound-system artists such as Coxsone Dodd and King Edwards, selling the records from the back of his car to Jamaicans who had moved to England. One of the first singles he sold was Marley's song, 'Judge Not', although his name was spelled wrongly as 'Morley' on the record. Little did either man know how important they were to become to each other a decade later.

During the 1960s, Blackwell's Island Records had become home for slightly left-field, progressive bands such as Traffic and by the 1970s, Island was the label of choice for artists wanting to pursue their careers but also maintain their musical integrity. Blackwell had already pursued Marley in 1967, only to find that Marley had just signed an agreement with Danny Sims. But by 1972, Marley was becoming dissatisfied with Sims' management. With Peter Tosh and Bunny Wailer, Marley went to visit Blackwell at the offices of Island Records on Basing Street, Notting Hill (near the large West Indian community living around All Saints Road), pointing out to him that The Wailers had never received any royalties for the Studio One recordings that Blackwell had distributed in Britain. Blackwell told them that he had paid thousands to their record label in Jamaica. At the news, Marley, Tosh and Wailer went up to the roof of the building and did what The Wailers normally did when considering important matters: they smoked marijuana. Meanwhile, Blackwell was downstairs, considering what to do with this group of intense men. He had been told that The Wailers were difficult but already Blackwell was coming to respect them. So, when he joined them on the roof, Blackwell proposed a most unusual deal. He would give The Wailers £4,000 to cover the cost of recording a new record and another £4,000 on the record's completion. What was more, at this stage there would be no contract. It was a handshake deal.

Blackwell was working on instinct. If he was wrong, there would be nothing to stop Marley and co walking off with the £4,000 and never coming back. To give some idea of just how big a gamble Blackwell was taking, £4,000 adjusted for inflation would be over £50,000 today. There were plenty of people who told Blackwell that he was throwing his money away, that The Wailers would disappear back to Jamaica with his money and that would be it, but Blackwell trusted his instincts. He was certain that The Wailers were something very special.

As important as the money, and the belief in them that it implied, was Blackwell's advice to Marley, Tosh and Wailer as to how they should move their career forward. In particular, The Wailers still presented themselves as a three-man vocal group, in line with such acts as The Temptations and The Four Tops. But tastes and listening habits were changing and already Blackwell was thinking on how to market The Wailers to the listening demographic he had nailed down: White fans of underground rock. To reach them, Blackwell needed a band that could tour and play live shows. So he told The Wailers to recruit a band, to rehearse and get tight; he would take care of the rest.

With Blackwell covering the cost of their airfares, The Wailers returned to Jamaica and set about recording what would be their first album for Island Records. Apart from Marley, Tosh and Wailer, the musicians involved included Aston and Carlton Barrett, Robbie Shakespeare on bass (who would go on to become a notable artist and producer in his own right) and Tyrone Downie on keyboards, while Marcia Griffiths and Rita Marley provided the backing vocals. By this time, the Marley marriage was under some strain, chiefly due to Bob's fathering of children with other women, but despite their differences the Marleys were always able to lay them aside to cooperate musically. Bob Marley wrote seven of the songs that would appear on *Catch a Fire*, with Tosh contributing two. As part of his plans to promote The Wailers, Blackwell ensured that a journalist from the British music paper, *Melody Maker*, was present for some of the recording sessions. In the 1970s in Britain, the music press was crucial when it came to breaking new acts: Blackwell was working hard to create the sort of critical buzz that would get word of mouth working on behalf of promoting The Wailers.

By the end of the year, The Wailers had finished recording the album. Marley flew to London with the master tapes to present them to Blackwell. Hearing them, Blackwell knew that his gamble had paid off – big time. This was an album to make the world take notice. His instincts vindicated, Blackwell and The Wailers signed a formal contract: from now on, Island Records would be promoting their career. It was Blackwell who also suggested the

HE LET THE MUSIC GROW AND THE MESSAGE FLOW.

- BOB MARLEY ON CHRIS BLACKWELL'S APPROACH

album title from a line in the song 'Slave Driver'. But while Blackwell, an aficionado of Jamaican music, loved the recording he also knew what would appeal to the ears of the underground rock fans he aimed to promote the band to. So, at the Island Records studios on Basing Street, Marley and Blackwell set about, as Blackwell called it, 'sweetening' the music for Western ears. Keyboards player John 'Rabbit' Bundrick added clavinet and synthesiser sounds to the record, their first use in reggae. But to really sweeten the record for Western ears, Blackwell needed some guitar: Wayne Perkins, from Alabama in the United States, was the man he brought in despite Perkins knowing next to nothing about reggae. But it would prove an inspired choice. Listen to 'Concrete Jungle', the first track on the album. Perkins opens with brilliantly phrased guitar over the top of Bundrick's clavinet, sounding almost as if it could be a new track from The Grateful Dead, and then the bass and drums kick the song into the reggae groove. Perkins got the solo on his third take. Marley was so delighted he ran into the recording studio and gave the guitarist a thanksgiving spliff.

Those present during these sessions affirm that Marley was very much part of the process involved in preparing the record for the market Blackwell had identified: this was no music-business Svengali remaking a band according to his own designs but a creative partnership, with Marley as ambitious to make it big as Blackwell. What was more, Blackwell was all for The Wailers espousing their Rastafarian faith in their music: he was personally sympathetic

OPPOSITE *Marley was prepared to do whatever it took to break through in the rest of the world.*

Credit: Alamy

MAIN *Bob Marley and the Wailers perform on the BBC's Old Grey Whistle Test in 1973.*

after his encounters with Rastas and, putting his business hat on, it gave a hook for the press coverage.

Catch a Fire was released in April 1973 to a press fanfare and solid – although not spectacular – sales. To follow up the release, The Wailers went on tour in Britain, starting in the same month. Mick Cater, their tour manager, recalled later that the only food they would eat during the tour was curry. When they came off stage after their first show, The Wailers were also puzzled by all the shouting from the audience: had they hated the show? They did not realise they were actually shouting for more. Mick Cater had to shove them back on stage for their encore. The tour ended with four nights at London's Speakeasy Club, then the hippest club in the country. The rock aristocracy turned out for the shows: Bryan Ferry, Eric Clapton, Jeff Beck, various members of The Who and Deep Purple, Brian Eno. They soon realised they were watching something new and revelatory.

Fresh from their UK tour, The Wailers went back into the studio to record the follow-up to *Catch a Fire*. They had already laid down the rhythm parts in Jamaica but *Burnin'* was completed at the Island Records' studio in Notting Hill. There were two recording studios in the building and, given the choice, The Wailers opted for the smaller one in the basement as it recorded the bass better. In a piece of rock trivia, while The Wailers recorded *Burnin'* downstairs, The Rolling Stones were recording *Goats Head Soup* upstairs. The first track on *Burnin'*

was 'Get Up, Stand Up', a stomping call to action jointly written by Bob Marley and Peter Tosh. The album also featured 'I Shot the Sheriff', which would become a huge hit for Eric Clapton when he recorded and released it in 1974, bringing more attention to the rapidly rising star of its writer, Bob Marley.

To further promote The Wailers and to start the long process of breaking them in the United States, Island Records arranged a tour for July 1973. But for Bunny Wailer, that was one tour too many and he told the other Wailers that he would not be going. When their work visa did not come through in time to get to the shows, the remaining Wailers – Marley, Tosh, Earl 'Wire' Lindo, Aston and Carlton Barrett, plus Joe Higgs to cover for Bunny Wailer – flew to Canada, crossing into America near Niagara Falls. In Boston, they played a week of three shows a night at a small jazz club called Paul's Mall. It was the sort of live apprenticeship that would serve the band very well in the years to come. Moving on to New York, the Wailers played for six nights at Max's Kansas City, sharing the bill with a young man from New Jersey, called Bruce Springsteen. He went on to some degree of success, too. The New York shows, heavily pushed by CBS Records who were touting their hot new star, were attended by the hippest New Yorkers with nary a Jamaican in sight. The band returned to Jamaica to recoup and recover during the summer but by October they were back on the road again, this time starting their new US tour on the West Coast in San Francisco. The Wailers were booked to play support for Sly and the Family Stone, the mixed-race funk rock pioneers fronted by Sly Stone and one of the biggest bands of the late psychedelic era. It should have been a perfect match but it turned into a disaster and The Wailers were kicked off the tour after four shows, finding themselves stranded in Las Vegas. The band played a handful of consolation shows and radio broadcasts, then flew to England in November for more touring.

England in November can be a grim, slate grey place for people brought up in Caribbean warmth and sunshine. The tour was mostly a slog through northern industrial towns, playing colleges and clubs, but it was never finished. Driving south from Leeds in the tour van, Tosh had a fit, brought on by a bad bout of flu. Arriving at the next venue in a snow storm, Tosh declared the tour doomed and booked himself on a flight back to Jamaica. The rest of the

tour had to be cancelled. Island Records, learning the lesson, made sure never to book The Wailers on a winter tour again.

Back in Jamaica, Wailer had built a home by the beach in Bull Bay in a Rastafarian community. Secure in his faith, Wailer had no wish to tour Babylon. Tosh was beginning to chafe at the prominence given to Marley's music in The Wailers' records. A fine songwriter himself, he had written only a couple of tracks on *Catch a Fire* and *Burnin'*. Meeting with Wailer, the two began talking about working together, without Marley. For his part, Marley was aware of the work that would be required to break through in the rest of the world. It was work he was prepared to do but his erstwhile bandmates didn't want to follow him. So, in 1974, Marley signed a new deal with Blackwell. Henceforth, Island Records would be promoting Bob Marley and the Wailers.

FAR LEFT *Bob Marley in concert around 1973.*

LEFT *Island Records boss Chris Blackwell had first tried to sign Bob Marley and the Wailers in 1967.*

RIGHT *There was some resentment among the band, and from Peter Tosh in particular, about Marley's prominence.*

HE WAS HUNGRY FOR MORE... FOR REACHING OTHER PARTS OF THE WORLD

- BLACKWELL ON MARLEY'S APPETITE FOR SUCCESS

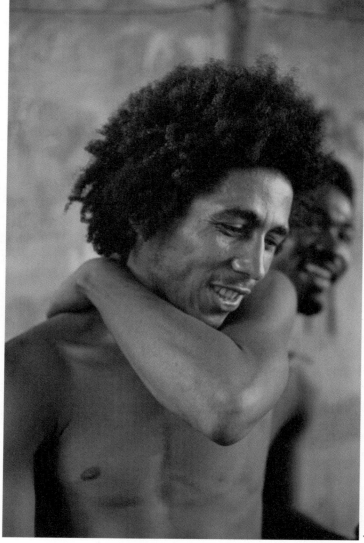

Credit: Alamy

TITLE:

CATCH A FIRE

| RELEASED: | APRIL 1973 | LENGTH: | 37:51 |

CATCH A FIRE MADE PEOPLE ALL OVER THE WORLD SIT UP AND TAKE NOTICE OF BOB MARLEY AND THE WAILERS, AND OF REGGAE MUSIC IN GENERAL

WITH *CATCH A FIRE*, THE band known then as simply The Wailers, created a bridge between the deep roots sound of Jamaica and the commercial rock music of the international market, particularly the USA and UK. Fronted by Bob Marley, Peter Tosh and Bunny Wailer and recorded between three different eight-track studios in Kingston, Jamaica, *Catch a Fire* was produced in London by Chris Blackwell of Island Records. The tracks – seven of which were composed by Marley and the other two by singer and lead guitarist, Peter Tosh – are a thoughtful and heartfelt collection, driven by a raw sense of urgency. When talking to Billboard in 1973, Marley compared his music to the blues saying, "It tells the truth from the people's viewpoint". In *Catch a Fire*, Marley and Tosh are courageous with their language and delivery, whether lamenting the oppression of Black people, calling for uprising from poverty or singing love songs. The original 20,000 pressed vinyl came in a sleeve, designed by graphic

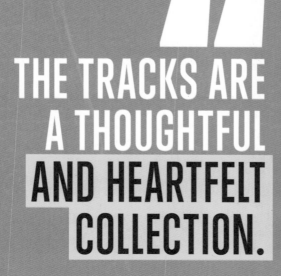

" THE TRACKS ARE A THOUGHTFUL AND HEARTFELT COLLECTION.

Credit: Getty Images

artist Rod Dyer, that depicted and functioned like a real Zippo lighter. Copies from that original pressing have since become a collector's item and the cover art was reproduced for the 2001 deluxe CD edition, which includes the original unreleased 'Jamaica version' of the album. *Catch a Fire* has become known as one of the greatest reggae albums of all time.

CONCRETE JUNGLE

'Concrete Jungle' features an uncharacteristically long introduction for a reggae song – easing rock fans in with familiar sounds of electric guitar,

ABOVE *Marley referenced his life and those of where he came from in his songs – a trait that stayed with him even as his success grew.*

LEFT *The lyrics on social injustice and encouraging people to improve the situation reached a whole new level when played live.*

before the thumping bass and classic reggae 'one drop' rhythm launches after 30 seconds. Later, it features a searing guitar solo from Muscle Shoals session guitarist, Wayne Perkins. The lyrics contain recognisable metaphors concerned with darkness and lightness, reminiscent of passages from the Bible and many aspects of both Caribbean and Western culture. 'Concrete Jungle' – or 'Jungle' for short – is the unofficial name of a notorious housing project built in the early 1970s on the edges of West Kingston's Trench Town. With this track, Marley gives a visceral commentary on the unhealthy aspects of urban life, as well as shining a light on the very real place where his friends lived.

SLAVE DRIVER

In 'Slave Driver', Marley and The Wailers continue to deliver a bold and meaningful message, giving a voice to some of their country's most marginalised people and acknowledging how racism continued to thrive within the structures of society. Yet the beautiful vocal harmonies created by Marley, Tosh and Wailer mean the listener might not even realise at first how political the song is. The title of the album – meaning 'go to hell' – comes from this track, and is sung in the background as Marley tells "slave drivers" with a calm certainty that "the table is turn'"and they're "gonna get burn" for their continued mistreatment of African people.

400 YEARS

Written and composed by Peter Tosh, previous versions of '400 Years' by The Wailers were already well known in Jamaica – particularly one produced by Lee 'Scratch' Perry. It's a haunting song of social criticism, referring to slavery in many forms and emphasising the relentlessness of oppression with the repeated "It's been four hundred years", in addition to the chilling backing vocals. Once again, the listener is asked to connect past and present atrocities together. But despite all of the horrendous references, there is also a hopeful side to the track with its reference to the biblical Genesis

BELOW *The inclusion of Wayne Perkins gave* Catch a Fire *a commercial rock element that opened up its potential audience.*

OPPOSITE Catch a Fire *was the first album with Island Records. Its owner, Chris Blackwell, wanted an international market, as did Marley.*

15, which holds the belief that after 400 years of mistreatment, liberation awaits.

STOP THAT TRAIN

The second track by Peter Tosh on the album, 'Stop That Train', is another indication of the success he would go on to have as a solo artist. The rich vocal harmonies by Marley and Wailer ensure this track stays in your head long after you've stopped listening to it. The listener can feel Tosh's sense of despair and heartbreak with lines like "even though I tried my best/I still don't find no happiness". It is an achingly sad subject matter, understood by many to be about someone contemplating suicide – or at least, somebody leaving a home they had once loved and tried to make better. But somehow, once again, the song seems to float and fade out with a sense of hope. In the last 15 seconds of the track, we hear Tosh mumble "it gotta be better".

BABY WE'VE GOT A DATE (ROCK IT BABY)

'Baby We've Got a Date (Rock It Baby)' is the first love song of the album, and it comes at the end of the first side of the original record – almost as something of a reward to new international listeners for sticking with the activism, and a promise of lighter content on the next side. It features another appearance from Wayne Perkins on the slide guitar, as well as backing vocals from Rita Marley and her friend Marcia Griffiths – a popular solo artist in

Credit: Alamy

CATCH A FIRE IS A BLAZING DEBUT.

- ROLLING STONE

music – funky guitar, congas, keyboards and that steady, rocking beat.

KINKY REGGAE

A laid-back, cheerful song that remained a firm fan favourite and was almost always played at Marley concerts. 'Kinky Reggae', following the lead of 'Stir It Up', is full of joy and demands the listener indulges in good times and some serious skanking. Fans have speculated about messages in Marley's lyrics in the track – it could be a coded story about drugs, a celebration of promiscuous sex or a secretive show of support for the queer community – but most critics agree that it's about somebody who can't settle down and that it's full of positive vibrations.

NO MORE TROUBLE

'No More Trouble' has few lyrics – the main ones being "We don't need no more trouble", repeated several times by Marley as well as in the soul-stirring harmonic backing vocals by Rita Marley and Marcia Griffiths. Its beauty and its power is in this evocative simplicity. A virtual collaboration with Erykah Badu was the first track on a 1999 remix album by hip-hop and rock artists, with production by Stephen Marley, called *Chant Down Babylon*.

MIDNIGHT RAVERS

Featuring a classic Aston 'Family Man' Barrett bass line pounding with conviction and driving the track forwards, 'Midnight Ravers' ends the album with a feeling of optimism and persistence. With the repeated "don't let me down!", Marley reminds the listeners that he's relying on them to help spread his music's message, and be a part of the positive change he sought to bring to the world.

Jamaica. This track has a mellow, positive feeling to it, and is about somebody who's looking forward to the date they have planned at "a quarter to eight".

STIR IT UP

This hypnotic track is another that was already well known in Jamaica as a Wailers track, and went on to become Marley's first successful song outside of his homeland. They first released 'Stir It Up' in 1967, and in 1972 American singer Johnny Nash released a cover version that scored a Top 15 hit in both the US and the UK – perhaps encouraging Marley to re-record it for the upcoming album. 'Stir It Up' also features Wayne Perkins, again, with a wah-wah-infused guitar lead. The lyrics are soothing and sensual and it's been said that Marley originally wrote the song for his wife, Rita. It's the longest song on the album – a smooth five minutes and 32 seconds of the irresistible classic elements of reggae

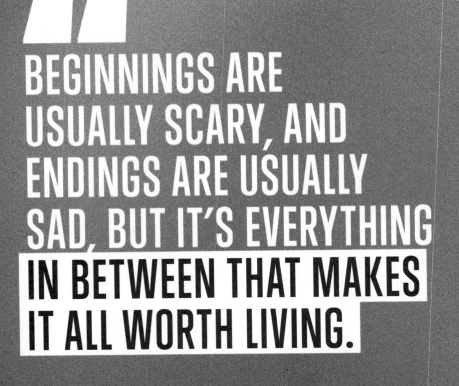

"BEGINNINGS ARE USUALLY SCARY, AND ENDINGS ARE USUALLY SAD, BUT IT'S EVERYTHING **IN BETWEEN THAT MAKES IT ALL WORTH LIVING.**

INSET *Bob Marley performing in Chicago, USA, in May 1978.*

TITLE:
BURNIN'

| RELEASED: | OCTOBER 1973 | LENGTH: | 38:28 |

BURNIN' RADIATES A COOL CONFIDENCE, UNAPOLOGETICALLY CALLING LISTENERS TOWARDS ACTION, REBELLION AND LOVE

BURNIN' WAS THE LAST ALBUM by The Wailers in their legendary original line-up, led by Bob Marley, Peter Tosh and Bunny Wailer and accompanied by keyboardist Earl 'Wire' Lindo, drummer Carlton Barrett and bassist Aston 'Family Man' Barrett. Although it was Marley who went on to achieve the most commercial success and popularity, both Tosh and Wailer would also rise to prominence and become legendary names in reggae music following their departure from the group. Alongside *Burnin's* defiant content, the simplicity of the writing keeps it accessible and somehow manages to cross boundaries of race, class and religion with its evocative imagery. In 1998, the *Burnin'* album cover inspired the artwork for *The Miseducation of Lauryn Hill* by American singer and rapper Lauryn Hill – one of the best-selling albums of all-time. The release of *Burnin'* was a definitive moment – showing Black people, amateur musicians, people from low-economic backgrounds and general social outsiders all around the world that it could be possible for them too to change the world, in some small way.

GET UP, STAND UP
One of the most well-known and well-loved Bob Marley songs, 'Get Up, Stand Up' was almost always played at live concerts – usually towards the end of the evening. It was also the last song Marley ever performed on stage. It was co-written with Peter Tosh and both him and Bunny Wailer later released solo versions – as did Marley – each with slightly different arrangements and takes on the third verse. While certainly continuing to draw from their feelings about political strife in Jamaica, Marley and Tosh wrote this song after touring Haiti and being deeply affected by witnessing the poverty there. The solid foundation of groove, combined with no-nonsense lyrical statements, made 'Get Up, Stand Up' transcend time and become an all-purpose, international human rights anthem.

HALLELUJAH TIME
Featuring lead vocals from Bunny Wailer, 'Hallelujah Time' is a lament about living on "borrowed time", but is also steeped in Rastafarian hopefulness. The unconventional harmonies in this track could be some of the most interesting achieved by the Marley, Wailer and Tosh vocal trio. It's softer than most of the other tracks on the album, with many lyrics that read like poetry, such as "But now it's not rain that water the cane crops/ But the sweat from man's brow/The substance from our spine". On the album notes, 'Hallelujah Time' is said to have been composed by Jean Watt, Wailer's wife. However, him and Marley were known to sometimes credit their compositions to others as a way of sharing royalties with their loved ones, for the long-term.

I SHOT THE SHERIFF
Another track from *Burnin'* that would go on to become one of Bob Marley's most popular and loved songs, 'I Shot the Sheriff' tells a story from the point of view of someone who's admitting to having killed a local sheriff, but denies also killing the deputy sheriff. Corruption in the Jamaican police force was rampant and The Wailers saw it as their duty to speak out against crooked institutions – especially those meant to serve the public – and encourage everyday people to defend themselves against violence, even if it came from people in a uniform. Later, in 1974, Marley explained the meaning of the song further: "I wanted to say 'I shot the police' but the government would have made a fuss so I said 'I shot the sheriff' instead… but it's the same idea: justice." The year after The Wailers' 'I Shot the Sheriff' release, Eric Clapton had a number one hit in the USA with a cover version.

  RIGHT *A portrait of Bob Marley taken in London in the year that* Burnin' *was released.*

Credit: Getty Images

BURNIN' AND LOOTIN'

'Burnin' and Lootin'' inspired the name of the album and takes the perspective of someone waking up as a captive, in the prison of society. Marley later said it was about "burning illusions", rather than material things. He talks about an unknown group taking him prisoner and describes them as "dressed in uniforms of brutality" – another strong message that is unfortunately still very relevant in many parts of the world today. Marley also references fellow reggae musician Jimmy Cliff's song 'Many Rivers to Cross', as he questions: "How many rivers do we have to cross/Before we can talk to the boss?".

PUT IT ON

The original of this track was first recorded by The Wailers in 1965 ('[I'm Gonna] Put It On'), in a ska style, on their debut album *The Wailing Wailers*, produced by Clement 'Coxsone' Dodd on the Studio One label. It was a hit in Jamaica, as was the soul arrangement released a few years later. 'Put It On' would go on to become one of Marley's most re-recorded songs. The lyrics are part prayer and part celebration and although there is a sorrowful tone throughout, hope and gratitude shine through.

SMALL AXE

There's been several different versions of 'Small Axe' recorded and released, with slight variations on the composition credits. The 1971 Jamaica issue credits the track to both Lee 'Scratch' Perry and Bob Marley, whereas *Burnin'*, and most later re-issues, credit only Marley. 'Small Axe' and the confusion over its credits are part of a larger feud involving The Wailers, Lee Perry and Island Records. The track has

THIS IS AS PERPLEXING AS IT IS JUBILANT.

- ROBERT CHRISTGAU

Credit: Getty Images

become known for its powerful metaphors about anti-colonial struggle, but Jamaican listeners could also hear the references to a more local, personal grievance that Marley had with the island's music industry. A group of three labels known as the 'Big Three' were dominating Jamaica's music business and with 'Small Axe', and lyrics such as "If you are the big tree/We are the small axe", Marley created an anthem of independence from the establishment.

PASS IT ON

The second track on the album that was written by Bunny Wailer and credited to his wife, Jean Watt, 'Pass It On' is one of the album's oldest songs – first written in the early 1960s, before the formation of

The Wailers. Opening with a sweet piano riff, the lyrics are filled with a soothing righteousness and preach living selflessly – "Live for yourself, you will live in vain/Live for others, you will live again".

DUPPY CONQUEROR

A version of 'Duppy Conqueror', produced by Lee 'Scratch' Perry, was released as a single in Jamaica in 1970 and appeared on The Wailers' *Soul Revolution*

ABOVE *Marley at the Island Records offices in Notting Hill. Burnin' was mixed at Island's studios.*

OPPOSITE *Bob Marley and the Wailers pose for a photo in London in 1973.*

other members of the band were Junior Marvin and Al Anderson on lead guitar, Tyrone Downie and Earl Lindo on keyboards, and Alvin 'Seeco' Patterson on percussion. Since 1970, the rhythm section had been made up of Aston 'Family Man' Barrett on bass, and his brother Carlton on drums. The brothers continued to be one of the most influential rhythm sections in reggae: Carlton Barrett had been instrumental in popularising the 'one drop' rhythm (in which the main snare hit comes on the third beat of the bar), which would become one of the foundational reggae rhythms, underpinning many of The Wailers' songs.

NATTY DREAD AND RASTAMAN VIBRATION

Natty Dread was the first album to be released with the new line-up. It was recorded at Harry J Studio in Kingston – at the time one of the most important recording studios in Jamaica – and released in October 1974. The record had moderate success overseas, particularly in the UK, where it reached number 43 in the charts. Like many of their subsequent albums, *Natty Dread* showcased Marley's ability to produce laid-back, upbeat tunes such as 'Lively Up Yourself' and 'Bend Down Low', as well as songs that were lyrically more sombre and addressed the difficult social conditions that were facing many Jamaicans. 'Them Belly Full (But We Hungry)' and

'3 O'Clock (Roadblock)', for instance, commented on the widespread hunger and poverty that affected many on the island, and the rapidly escalating social unrest that this was leading to.

The title and album cover – which featured a headshot of Marley growing out his dreadlocks – were also significant. Rastafari, both as a religious movement, but also as a style and culture, was still looked down upon by many conservative Jamaicans. Yet here was a prominent musician proudly displaying his adherence to the faith, and producing music that would increasingly cut across social and racial lines while he did it.

Following the release of *Natty Dread*, the band embarked on one of its first major international tours in the summer of 1975. Beginning in May in Miami, it took in a number of American and Canadian cities, before heading to the UK. The British leg of the tour included Manchester and Birmingham, but it began in London, where the band would play two of its pivotal live shows at the Lyceum Theatre, over the nights of 18 and 19 July. The performances would be immortalised in the album *Live!*, which was recorded using a mobile studio belonging to The Rolling Stones. With little in the way of post-production, the album was one of the bands' rawest recordings, featuring a rapturous rendition of the audience singing along to 'No

Woman, No Cry', which was their breakout single from that year, reaching 22 in the UK charts.

Natty Dread was quickly followed up by *Rastaman Vibration* in the spring of 1976, which was already the band's eighth studio album. Like *Natty Dread*, the LP featured a mix of upbeat tunes (such as 'Positive Vibration' and 'Roots Rock Reggae'), as well as songs that demonstrated a far more urgent and militant political sensibility, for example 'Crazy Baldheads' and 'War'. The latter would prove to be particularly prophetic. It featured quotes from a speech by Haile Selassie – Emperor of Ethiopia and God incarnate for followers of Rastafari – which spoke of unceasing conflict around the world if racial discrimination was allowed to continue. 'War' was also one of the first tracks illustrating Marley's increasingly Pan-African politics, particularly his connection to the liberation movements of southern Africa. The track speaks of the "ignoble and unhappy regimes" oppressing the people of Angola, Mozambique and South Africa, and shortly after the record was released, in June of 1976, hundreds of Black students from Soweto, one of the largest townships in South Africa, were gunned down by police during a protest against Afrikaans being introduced into the school curriculum.

AMBUSH IN THE NIGHT

'War' was prophetic in other ways as well: by 1976, the political situation in Jamaica was intensifying rapidly and bloody gun battles between rival gangs was becoming a daily occurrence. Jamaica had only gained independence from Britain in August 1962, and the country was in a fragile state, with crumbling infrastructure and shortages of food and other essentials. The pre-colonial social order had also remained largely intact: a small elite of White Jamaicans (as well as some of mixed heritage) still ruled the country, while widespread poverty was a daily reality for much of the Black population.

Within this context, a sharp division emerged between the two dominant political parties – the left-wing People's National Party (PNP), led by Michael Manley, and the conservative Jamaican Labour Party (JLP), led by Edward Seaga. Though

ABOVE *The soulful harmonies provided by the I Threes elevated the music of The Wailers to something beyond pure reggae.*

FAR LEFT *Aston 'Family Man' Barrett, seen here backstage with Marley, played bass on most of The Wailers' releases.*

LEFT *The other Barrett brother, Carlton, took care of the drums, and was responsible for popularising the 'one drop' rhythm.*

Credit: Getty Images

"WHEN I SEE THE YOUTH FIGHTING AGAINST THE YOUTH FOR THE POLITICIANS, I REALLY FEEL SICK.

– BOB MARLEY ON JAMAICA'S POLITICAL UNREST

Manley had come from an elite family, he had a background in trade union organising and journalism, and identified with the struggles of poor and working-class Jamaicans, adapting his style and dress sense in a way that was at odds with the elite social codes of the time. First coming to power in 1972, Manley adopted a democratic socialist platform that saw him form alliances with other socialist countries in the region, particularly Cuba.

Seaga, on the other hand, was much more closely tied with the financial interests of the traditional Jamaican elite. As such, his party received substantial support from the US, in particular from the CIA, who had a long history of intervention in Latin America and the Caribbean in order to prevent the spread of socialism. PNP supporters even went so far as to dub Seaga 'Ciaga', for his perceived role as a US stooge. Critics of the PNP, meanwhile, saw the party as merely a front for Soviet interests.

This proxy war became particularly vicious in Jamaica, with both parties coming to rely on the

 LEFT *56 Hope Road was a refuge not just for Marley, but friends and young people seeking shelter from the violence.*

CHAPTER FOUR

OPPOSITE *Marley eventually left his beloved home in 1976, taking a period of self-imposed exile.*

RIGHT *The UK tour in 1975 to promote* Natty Dread *would produce the sublime* Live! *album.*

BELOW LEFT *Michael Manley enjoyed an easy re-election for the PNP following the Smile Jamaica concert.*

BELOW RIGHT *Edward Seaga of the JLP represented the elite, conservative Jamaica.*

support of heavily armed gangs, led by 'dons' who controlled the streets of much of the capital. Large parts of Kingston were organised into 'garrisons', neighbourhoods that were strongholds of one of the political parties. For instance, Trench Town, where Bob Marley had grown up, was known as a PNP-affiliated area, whereas the rival neighbourhood of Tivoli Gardens became a JLP stronghold.

Bob Marley had initially been a supporter of Manley's PNP, but as the level of violence intensified, he attempted to occupy a neutral position in the conflict. In 1975, he purchased a former colonial mansion at 56 Hope Road in uptown Kingston. He had intended to make his new home, which had around 12 bedrooms, a safe haven, not only for his band members, who used it as a rehearsal space, but for the many disaffected young people who would congregate around Marley, seeking support and a

refuge from the violence. Despite this intention, 56 Hope Road would in fact turn out to be the site of one the bleakest moments in his life.

In an attempt to quell the violence, the Jamaican Ministry of Culture had proposed a concert, dubbed Smile Jamaica, which would take place at the end of 1976. Bob Marley was approached to headline it, as he was seen as the only national figure who might be able to unite the warring factions. Marley agreed to play, on the assumption that the concert would not be aligned with either party. But with Marley on board, the PNP made the cynical decision of bringing the national elections forward to 15 December, ten days after the concert. What had begun as a well-intentioned move to unite the country soon made Marley look like he had been co-opted by the government.

He started to receive death threats almost as soon as the concert was announced. On the night of 3 December 1976, while The Wailers were rehearsing for the concert at Marley's home, two carloads of gunmen stormed through the gates of the building, ran into the house and opened fire. Several people were shot including Don Taylor, The Wailers' manager, who was hit five times in the legs; Marley's friend Lewis Griffith; Rita Marley, who was very nearly killed, a bullet leaving a bloody graze across her forehead; and Bob Marley himself, who was shot across the chest, the bullet lodging in his left arm. Miraculously all four survived, but the trauma of the event shaped much of the remainder of Marley's life.

The gunmen were never found and no one was prosecuted for the attack. Since that moment, the assassination attempt has been shrouded in mystery and conspiracy theories. Jamaican novelist Marlon James even wrote an epic novel, *A Brief History of Seven Killings*, exploring the event from various angles. Some have speculated the hit was revenge over gambling debts owed by Marley's friend, footballer Allan 'Skill' Cole, who had allegedly fixed a horse race, while others have put forward the idea that it was carried out by a rival faction within the PNP in order to further stoke tensions. However, most of the evidence has come to support the theory that gunmen aligned with the JLP were responsible for carrying out the hit.

Going against the advice of family and friends, Bob Marley and the Wailers did in fact play at Smile Jamaica, which took place in Kingston's National Heroes Park. The turnout defied expectations, with as many as 80,000 people attending the gig. The Wailers were on stage for well over an hour, playing tracks including 'War', 'Get Up, Stand Up' and 'Rat Race'. Upon leaving the stage, Marley opened up his shirt to reveal the scars on his chest and arms. As predicted, the success of the concert worked in favour of Manley, who was re-elected at the end of 1976 with a majority, but it did little to quell the political violence, which continued to flare up for the rest of decade. For Marley, it marked a significant turning point: the very next day, he and the rest of The Wailers boarded a plane for Nassau, in the Bahamas, where they would stay for the remainder of the year. Thereafter, Marley would fly on to London, where he went into a period of self-imposed exile. He did not return to Jamaica until 1978.

TITLE:

NATTY DREAD

RELEASED:	OCTOBER 1974	LENGTH:	38:59

MARLEY STEPS INTO A FRONTMAN ROLE WITH EASE ON NATTY DREAD, AND HIS SONGWRITING SKILLS SHINE BRIGHT

NATTY DREAD WAS MARLEY'S FIRST ALBUM following the departure of Peter Tosh and Bunny Wailer, and the first release as Bob Marley and the Wailers. The Wailers Band also had some new additions, including Junior Marvin and Al Anderson on lead guitar and the I Threes on backing vocals – made up of Rita Marley, Marcia Griffiths and Judy Mowatt. The richness of the new line-up creates a pleasing balance of the traditional, down-to-earth Wailers sound and the influence of pop and rock music. Now the undisputed lead songwriter of the group, Marley continues in his lyrical style of blending personal experiences with political statements, encouraging listeners to make connections between the struggles of an individual and the oppressive structures within society. Despite the weight of the subjects it explores, *Natty Dread* also manages to retain The

BELOW *Al Anderson and Bob Marley photographed at the Odeon, Birmingham, during their 1975 UK tour.*

OPPOSITE *Junior Marvin, along with Marcia Griffiths and Rita Marley of the I Threes photographed in America.*

Credit: Getty Images

Wailers' signature laid-back feel, creating a relaxed atmosphere even among hard-hitting messages that no doubt terrified some members of Jamaica's political and economic elite at the time. Of course, *Natty Dread* is also steeped in spirituality, Rastafari righteousness and a persistent and gloriously infectious optimism.

LIVELY UP YOURSELF

Setting up the album with a perfect opener, 'Lively Up Yourself' begins with an insistently unforgettable bass line from Aston 'Family Man' Barrett and a background wail from Marley. A different version of the song was originally released as a Wailers single in 1971 and was a hit in Jamaica. Built upon a nonchalant reggae beat, the lyrics are the most carefree of the record with the title phrase of "Lively up yourself/And don't be no drag" repeated frequently throughout. Anderson's meticulous guitar riffs assist the tune in gliding along and creating a real good-time feel. 'Lively Up Yourself' became a popular track at live Marley concerts for many years to come, and was guaranteed to get the crowd skanking and singing along.

NO WOMAN, NO CRY

'No Woman, No Cry' is probably the most well-known song on the album, but it was the live version from the 1975 *Live!* album that became a huge

worldwide hit. The *Natty Dread* studio version uses a drum machine and has a faster tempo with some almost rap-like vocal delivery from Marley. It's a nostalgic track, with lyrics that look back fondly on growing up in "a government yard in Trench Town". The title and main refrain comes from Jamaican patois and translates into English as 'woman, don't cry' – the second 'no' actually being 'nuh' – but is sometimes misunderstood outside of Jamaica to mean 'if there is no woman, there is no reason to

NATTY DREAD IS MULTIFACETED REBEL MUSIC.

– ROLLING STONE

cry'. On the contrary, Marley seems to be singing this song to a woman he loves ("Little darling, don't shed no tears") and is trying to cheer her up by recounting fond memories of the good old days.

THEM BELLY FULL (BUT WE HUNGRY)

The I Threes shine in 'Them Belly Full (But We Hungry)', introducing the melody and softly moving the song along with their heartfelt echoes of Marley's words. Ever the prophet, Marley highlights the divide between rich and poor and warns "a hungry mob is an angry mob", blending these important messages effortlessly with his hopeful style as he encourages people to "Forget your troubles and dance". The simplicity of the repeated refrain "Them belly full but we hungry" makes it all the more compelling, and the melodic lengthening of the word 'hungry' makes the message impossible to ignore.

REBEL MUSIC (3 O'CLOCK ROADBLOCK)

The eerie and emotive backing melodies by the I Threes and the bluesy harmonica by Lee Jaffe add a new dimension to The Wailers' sound in 'Rebel Music (3 O'clock Roadblock)'. The lyrics tell the story of police harassment, with a casual commentary on the restrictions and expectations placed on the general public by law enforcement. It is said to have been written after Marley was stopped by a night-time police car check, and the lyrics end on "Hey Mr Cop/Ain't got no birth certificate on me now." Despite the serious content, the track is rocked along by a sensuous rhythm that cries out to be danced to.

SO JAH SEH

'So Jah Seh' was the only single released from *Natty Dread* – although there are certainly a few other tracks that became live favourites or bigger hits in different versions. A spiritual song, with an other-worldly feel, 'So Jah Seh' references passages from the Bible, along with Rastafari concepts such as 'I and I' – the belief that all people are one under Jah, so instead of 'you and me' or 'we', it is 'I and I'.

NATTY DREAD

The title track is one of the more playful on the album, inspired by Marley's dreads – the increased length of which had earned him the nickname 'Natty Dread' from some friends and fans in Jamaica. The lyrics are an exploration of a neighbourhood in Kingston through Marley's eyes. 'Natty Dread' became a popular sing-along track at live shows.

BEND DOWN LOW

Smooth and suggestive, 'Bend Down Low' confirms Marley's reputation for having a romantic

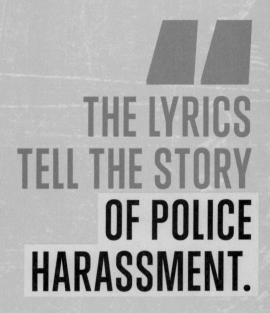

THE LYRICS TELL THE STORY OF POLICE HARASSMENT.

and sensual character. A different version was first released in Jamaica in 1966 as a single, in collaboration with The Soul Brothers. The version of the song on this album feels lightweight and cheeky, with the characteristically soulful backing vocals from the I Threes doing wonders in enhancing the summery feel-good mood.

TALKIN' BLUES

In 'Talkin' Blues', we hear Marley embrace the influence of American pop music while still managing to stay true to his reggae roots and his focus on social commentary and political statements. Earlier in the album, Marley described experiences of injustice and expressed frustration with oppressive structures and figures. In this track, he steps the criticism up a notch with some lyrics sounding like a call for direct action ("Cause I feel like bombin' a church/Now that you know that the preacher is lyin") and topped off with wailing bluesy harmonica from Lee Jaffe and haunting call-and-response vocal arrangements.

REVOLUTION

Full of emotion, 'Revolution' condemns greed and demands freedom for all with lyrics like "My friend, I wish that you could see/Like a bird in the tree, the prisoners must be free." The strength in the words of this track, and the whole album, is even more impressive when we consider that, at the time, popular rock music was heading towards a disco era. Marley ends 'Revolution', and the *Natty Dread* album, with ever-hopeful imagery of a Rasta utopia: "Let righteousness cover the earth/Like the water cover the sea, yeah!"

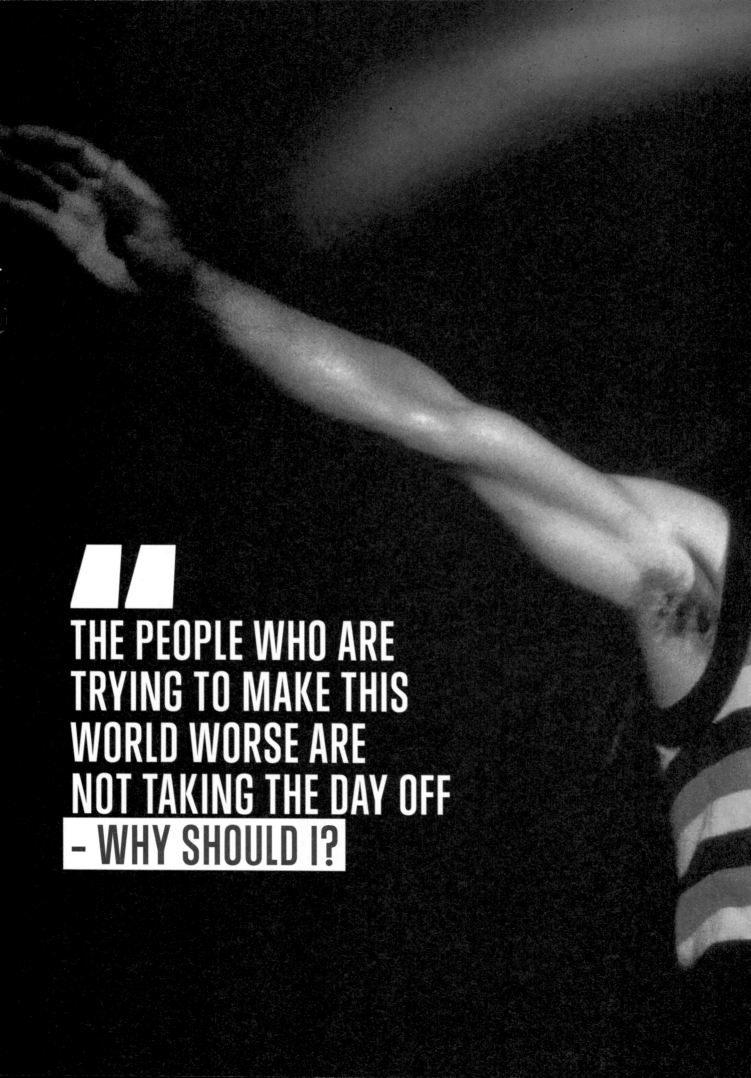

"
THE PEOPLE WHO ARE
TRYING TO MAKE THIS
WORLD WORSE ARE
NOT TAKING THE DAY OFF
– WHY SHOULD I?

NIGHT SHIFT

The opening lines of 'Night Shift' ("The sun shall not smite I by day/Nor the moon by night, no") are almost a direct quote from the Bible (Psalm 121:6) widely understood to mean that God (or Jah) will protect people from all, even the dangers of day and the night. But the song is primarily about Marley's experiences of working a night shift at a car factory during the short period of time that he lived with his mother in Delaware, USA, in 1966. 'Night Shift' is another remake of an old Wailers recording, 'It's Alright', which was produced by Lee 'Scratch' Perry in 1970 and released on compilations in the 1990s.

WAR

Marley's dedication to the aspiration of a Rastafari revolution is most evident on this particular album in the penultimate track, 'War'. The lyrics are almost entirely taken from a speech given by Ethiopian Emperor Haile Selassie I at the United Nations General Assembly in 1963, with extended complex sentences (eg "Until the philosophy which holds one race superior and another inferior/Is finally and permanently discredited and abandoned/Everywhere is war") skilfully crafted into poetry. The deep and disciplined rhythm section, held down expertly by the Barrett brothers, supports the rising tension that builds throughout the track and finds a release with the repeat of the simple vocal hook, "War".

RAT RACE

The tenacious and politically charged 'Rat Race' is about exactly what you'd expect it to be about – Marley's frustration with the competitive lifestyle and capitalist systems that he'd witnessed in the USA and Europe. He voices his discontentment with the experience of seeing these same unequal systems playing out in his homeland, and alludes to corruption within Jamaica's politicians and police force, while also making it known that he did not wish to be involved – "Political violence fill ya city, yeah!/Don't involve Rasta in your say say/Rasta don't work for no CIA". Marley ends *Rastaman Vibration* with a potent and sincere message, leaving listeners wondering what he's going to say next time.

Credit: Alamy

LEFT *While* Rastaman Vibration *opens with the optimistic 'Positive Vibration', the album retains all the power of previous releases.*

ABOVE *Marley on stage in the Netherlands on the European leg of the Rastaman Vibration Tour.*

" IT ENDS WITH A POTENT, SINCERE MESSAGE

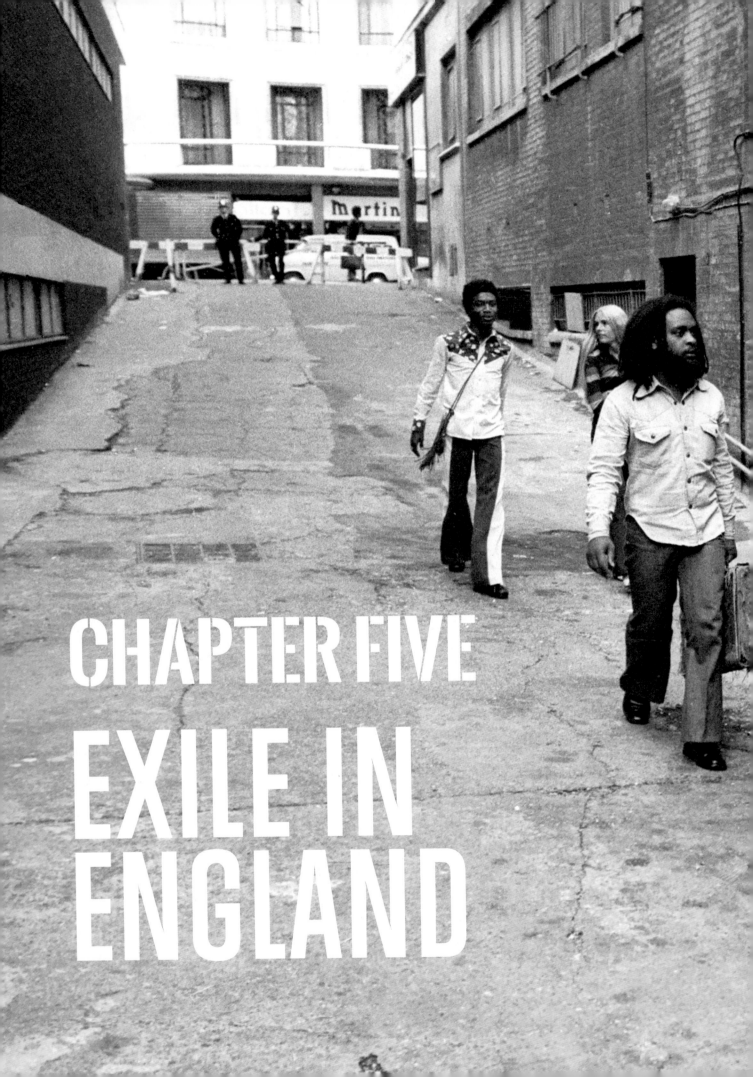

CHAPTER FIVE
EXILE IN ENGLAND

EXILE IN ENGLAND

Bob Marley's exile in London coincided with a period of cultural and political upheaval and would prove to be one of his most creative chapters

WORDS BY **ADAM QUARSHIE**

B ob Marley arrived in London at the start of 1977. His self-imposed exile in England had come about from a deep sense of sorrow and disillusion with the violence that was engulfing Jamaica, which had culminated in the attempt on his life in December 1976. But rather than falling into despair, his time in London proved to be extremely fruitful: in less than two years, he recorded two studio albums – one of which, *Exodus*, is regarded by many to be his finest – embarked on two major tours and headlined another concert in Jamaica designed to bring an end to the political conflict once and for all. By the end of the 1970s, Bob Marley had been transformed from a local singer from the backstreets of Kingston to the first superstar from the Global South, one whose vision would inspire downtrodden people across the world.

LIFE IN LONDON

While in London, Marley and his entourage moved between several houses and stayed with various friends and acquaintances. The first house he lived in was 42 Oakley Street in Chelsea, where he would spend around nine months. It was at this address that he recuperated from the shock of the assassination attempt and where he would pen the first songs attempting to make sense of the trauma. During this time, he fell into a relationship with

Cindy Breakspeare, a fellow Jamaican who had been crowned Miss World in November 1976. Though still married to Rita Marley, Breakspeare was one of several other women Bob had relationships with and fathered children with; she gave birth to their son Damian in 1978.

Following his time at the Oakley Street house (which was given a blue plaque highlighting its historical significance in 2019) he lived at another Chelsea address, Old Church Street, and also spent time in the South London neighbourhoods of Kennington and Brixton. During his downtime, Marley and the rest of The Wailers would often be seen playing football in Battersea Park.

A PUNKY REGGAE PARTY

Though 1970s London was markedly less violent than Kingston, the city was nonetheless going through significant social and political convulsions of its own, with racial tensions in particular bubbling to the surface. At the Notting Hill Carnival in August 1976, there was a huge uprising in response to heavy-handed policing, the culmination of a buildup of hostility between London's Black communities and the Metropolitan Police, who were known to target, harass and intimidate young Black people. This period also saw the rise of the National Front, a racist organisation who opposed immigration from Britain's former colonies. Their marches through

London's multicultural neighbourhoods were often met with large counter-demonstrations.

Marley's arrival in London also coincided with a period of intense creativity in the city's music scene. Cultural alliances were forming in resistance to the rising tide of racism, particularly between reggae musicians and the burgeoning punk scene, united by their shared outsider status and anti-establishment politics. In response to racist comments made by a number of prominent musicians, including Eric Clapton, who had expressed support for the xenophobic Conservative politician Enoch Powell – and who had ironically covered Marley's '1 Shot the Sheriff' in 1975 – a group of grassroots activists formed Rock Against Racism and organised anti-racism gigs across the country, featuring multiracial line-ups of prominent punk and reggae bands including The Clash, The Slits, X-Ray Spex, Steel Pulse and Misty in Roots.

One of the key figures to unite these two worlds, and the first person to introduce Bob Marley to the punk scene, was Don Letts. Born in London to parents who had migrated from Jamaica as part of the Windrush Generation, Letts was the manager of clothing store Acme Attractions on Chelsea's King's Road, which was round the corner from where Marley lived at the time. The shop was popular with punks, who Letts introduced to dub and reggae, which he blasted from the shop's sound system all day long. According to Letts, he had first met Marley after his legendary gig at the Lyceum Theatre in

1975. Though Marley had initially been unimpressed with the 'nasty punk rockers', he would nonetheless go on to write the hit 'Punky Reggae Party', which tipped its hat to the subcultural affinity between the two movements, and name-checked many of the era's key players. Letts would go on to become a vital chronicler of the punk scene, working as a filmmaker, photographer and DJ, and even featuring on the cover of The Clash's *Black Market Clash*, marching defiantly towards a line of police.

EXODUS AND KAYA

'Punky Reggae Party' would be released in the summer of 1977 as a B-side to 'Jamming', which appeared on *Exodus*. The album proved to be the pivotal recording from Marley's time in London, and became one of his most powerful musical statements, showcasing the huge breadth of Marley's skills as a songwriter. On the one hand, it was a deeply personal and heartfelt record which channelled the pain and anger that Marley had accumulated over the previous few months. But as well as being a statement of defiance in the face of violence and adversity, it was also infused with warmth and joy. It would go on to be widely regarded as Marley's masterpiece, and would even be named album of the century by *Time* magazine in 1999.

The tracks that made up *Exodus* were all recorded between January and April 1977, illustrating the fact that the band had got straight to work as soon as they'd landed in London. The LP was

recorded at Island's Basing Street Studios in Ladbroke Grove, another neighbourhood where Marley spent a lot of time due to the connections he forged with the area's Caribbean community. The first side of the album provided a sense of catharsis from having survived an attempted murder. 'So Much Things to Say' spoke of the betrayal of Jamaican heroes, while 'Guiltiness' and 'The Heathen' spoke in fiery tones of the fates that would befall those whose lives had been given over to treachery. The title track 'Exodus' was almost transcendent in its vision – connecting Marley's flight from Jamaica with the Rasta quest for a spiritual return to Africa, which also managed to riff one of the PNP's slogans ("We know where we're going"). The second part of the album, meanwhile, had an altogether different tone, featuring the extremely upbeat 'Three Little Birds' and love

songs such as 'Turn Your Lights Down Low' and 'Jamming', showing that Marley could often write a revolutionary song and a love song in the same day.

To promote the album, Bob Marley and the Wailers embarked on a major European tour from May to June 1977. The Exodus Tour culminated in London at Finsbury Park's Rainbow Theatre. However, the two final London dates had to be cancelled after Marley hurt his toe while playing football. At the time, it seemed like a relatively minor injury, but it would later transpire to be something far worse, with devastating consequences.

After returning from the tour, Marley and The Wailers headed straight back into the studio. Their second LP to be recorded in London – *Kaya* – was released in March 1978, barely six months after the release of *Exodus*. Though the album featured some of his best-loved songs, such as 'Is This

TOP LEFT *Bob Marley brings the leaders of Jamaica's warring parties together at the One Love Peace Concert in 1978.*

RIGHT *A portrait of Bob taken at a hotel in London in February 1978.*

BELOW *Bob and Rita Marley pictured at The Daisy, an exclusive disco in Beverly Hills, California, in July 1978.*

Credit: Getty Images

INSET *Bob playing guitar in a London hotel room in February 1978, around the time he was recording* Kaya.

Credit: Getty Images

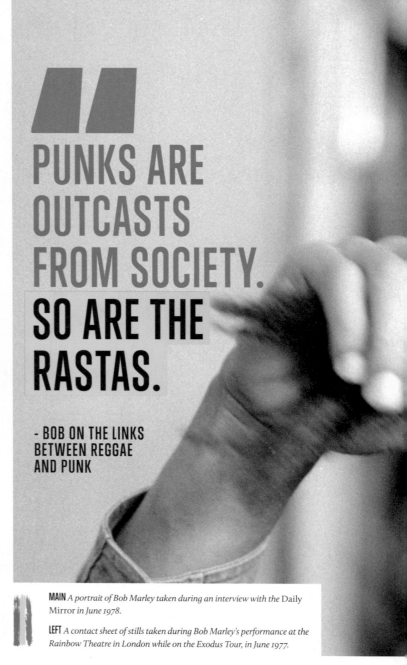

" PUNKS ARE OUTCASTS FROM SOCIETY. SO ARE THE RASTAS.

- BOB ON THE LINKS BETWEEN REGGAE AND PUNK

MAIN *A portrait of Bob Marley taken during an interview with the* Daily Mirror *in June 1978.*

LEFT *A contact sheet of stills taken during Bob Marley's performance at the Rainbow Theatre in London while on the Exodus Tour, in June 1977.*

Love', as well as some beautiful arrangements on tracks like 'She's Gone', it was, in many respects, a surprising follow-up to *Exodus*. Largely stripped of the political and social commentary that had been so artfully chronicled on The Wailers' earlier work, *Kaya* was instead a more hedonistic offering, focusing on the pleasures of sun, relationships, and copious consumption of weed. Marley's formidable weed-smoking abilities were no secret by then; he'd been arrested and fined for cannabis possession a year earlier. But the album's laid-back vibe, and its unapologetic celebration of ganja (after which the album was named), stood in contrast to the pleas against suffering and injustice that had been such a core component of his earlier work. *Kaya* demonstrated the contradictions and duality of Marley as a superstar: on the one hand there was

Marley the militant Pan-Africanist and prophet of Rastafari; on the other hand, there was Marley the crowd-pleaser, singing about sunshine and weed in a way that made him a stoner pin-up as much as a revolutionary musician.

The release of *Kaya* heralded other monumental changes in Marley's personal and political life. In 1977, he learned that his toe 'injury' he thought he had sustained while playing football was in fact a malignant form of cancer, acral lentiginous melanoma. He was immediately advised by doctors to take serious action, which might have necessitated the amputation of his toe. But for reasons best known to himself – possibly distrust of the medical establishment partly born of his religious convictions – he chose to ignore this advice and instead went to a Miami hospital to have some of the

cancerous tissue removed, followed by a skin graft. It was a patch-up job that did little to address the issue. Left unchecked, the cancer would spread rapidly throughout his body over the coming years.

RETURNING TO JAMAICA

In the spring of 1978, a full 16 months after he'd first left Jamaica, circumstances conspired to thrust Marley back into the centre of the political conflict that had been ravaging his home country. Following the Smile Jamaica Concert in 1976, little had changed to reduce the level of violence and animosity between Kingston's politically affiliated gangs. In 1974, Jamaican Prime Minister Michael Manley had introduced controversial Gun Courts in an attempt to halt the lethal wave of gun violence. Anyone found in possession of weapons or ammunition was tried

Credit: Alamy

OPPOSITE *From May to August 1978, Bob and The Wailers performed across the United States, Canada and Europe for the Kaya Tour.*

ABOVE *In 2019, a blue English Heritage plaque was unveiled at 42 Oakley Street, Chelsea, where Marley lived for a short time in 1977.*

without a jury and, if convicted, sent to jail. In 1978, two of those charged in this manner, who happened to find themselves imprisoned at the same time, were gang leaders Aston 'Bucky Marshall' Thompson, don of a PNP gang, and Claudius 'Claudie' Massop, don of a JLP-affiliated gang. Rendered temporarily powerless by their time inside, the two men decided to sign a 'peace treaty' in order to halt the conflict between their respective sides. Upon his release, Massop flew to London to meet with Marley, determined to bring him back to Jamaica in order to headline another peace concert. The gravity of the Jamaican political situation was such that many believed that Bob Marley was the only person with enough clout to heal the country's collective wounds.

On 22 April 1978, Bob Marley and the Wailers once again took to the stage in their home city, this time playing to over 30,000 fans at Kingston's National Stadium at what was dubbed the One Love Peace Concert. The Wailers played alongside a number of other prominent reggae acts, including Jacob Miller and Inner Circle, Althea and Donna, Big Youth, Dennis Brown, as well as former Wailers Peter Tosh and Bunny Wailer. During their headline set, with Marley leaping and whirling around the stage during a rendition of 'Jamming', he called upon the JLP leader, Edward Seaga, to come up to the stage, followed (after a bit of hesitation) by Michael

Manley. In what was to become a historic moment and a potent gesture towards unity in Jamaican politics, Marley held the two rivals' hands together while the band continued to play, a plea for peace in a country that was in a state of near civil war.

While it was an impressive gesture, its effects were short-lived as the political violence continued; both Bucky Marshall and Claudie Massop, alongside hundreds of others involved in the conflict, were gunned down the following year. The violence would continue until the eventual inauguration of Seaga in 1980, and would plague Jamaica for decades to come.

BACK ON THE ROAD

Almost as soon as The Wailers had finished the concert, they were back on tour, this time across Europe and North America to promote *Kaya*. Yet another live album came from these travels: *Babylon By Bus* was released in November 1978, with most recordings taken from live shows at the Pavillon de Paris in June of that year. Firmly established now as reggae's foremost superstar, and increasingly seen as a spokesperson for the oppressed worldwide, Marley did a huge amount of travelling that year. But in 1979 and 1980, in what was to be the final chapter of his life, it was increasingly to Africa, and the struggles for liberation in the south of the continent, that Marley would turn his attention.

TITLE:
EXODUS

RELEASED:	JUNE 1977	LENGTH:	37:24

AN ALBUM OF TWO PARTS, EXODUS STRIKES AN IMPRESSIVE BALANCE BETWEEN UNCOMPROMISING POLITICAL CALLS-TO-ARMS AND PASSIONATE ROMANCE

WIDELY CONSIDERED TO BE HIS best album, there are more tracks from *Exodus* on the acclaimed Marley greatest hits collection, *Legend* (1984) – the highest-selling reggae album of all time – than any of his other records. Released just six months after Marley and his wife, Rita, were injured in an assassination attempt in Jamaica, *Exodus* was recorded in London, where Marley had found refuge from the political violence happening in his homeland. The two sides of *Exodus* are thematically very different, with the stories of the first five songs revolving around politics and social justice, and the second half of the album focusing more on sex, love and good times. Motifs of spirituality run throughout, and the five tracks on the second side became five of Marley's most popular songs. With more of an emphasis on piano, trumpet and guitar than on previous albums, even the tracks that tackle difficult topics seem to have a joyous and celebratory lift. Vocally, Marley's approach is minimal, but full of emotion. Exodus is a rare find – an album that is both socially and politically conscious, but also makes people get up and dance. It was Marley's biggest-selling studio album, and has reached Gold status in the USA, UK and Canada.

NATURAL MYSTIC

'Natural Mystic' opens up the album with a deep, rumbling bass line under a lightly skanking rhythm guitar that slowly fades in, building a dramatic tension, until the pounding drums and Marley's melancholy vocals kick in after 30 seconds. The subject matter is somewhat despairing; an exploration of the human condition and life's

RIGHT *The Exodus Tour was cut short after Marley suffered a serious toe injury while playing football.*

OPPOSITE Exodus *was named the best album of the 20th century by* Time *magazine in 1999.*

Credit: Getty Images

injustices with some heart-wrenching apocalyptic allusions, such as "This could be the first trumpet/ Might as well be the last/Many more will have to suffer/Many more will have to die/Don't ask me why". But with the sonorous horn arrangements and plenty of guitar adornments, the feel of the track is not a sombre one.

SO MUCH THINGS TO SAY

In 'So Much Things to Say', Marley seems to be referring directly to his recent assassination attempt and comparing his experiences to that of other freedom fighters he admires: "I'll never forget no way/They crucified Jesus Christ/I'll never forget no way/They sold Marcus Garvey for rice/I'll never forget no way/They turned their back on Paul Bogle". The track has an upbeat feel, with a funk influence evident in the main riff and the I Threes' backing vocals cushioning Marley's foreboding and captivating campaign against "spiritual wickedness in high and low places". 'So Much Things To Say' wraps up with Marley singing fast, in a scat-like style, ending abruptly on "They got the rumour without humour/They don't know what they're doin', yeah!"

GUILTINESS

With dramatically delivered opening lines ("Guiltiness/Pressed on their conscience") that sound like a karmic warning to the people who ordered the shooting of Marley six months previously, 'Guiltiness' is anchored by another mighty Barrett bass line, punctuated by foreboding horns and packed out with some dense percussion. Over all of this, Marley delivers a straightforward and sobering message, decrying self-serving people in power who "...do anything/To materialise their every wish" rather than attending to the needs of the people. "These are the big fish/Who always try to eat down the small fish" spoke to people at the time, and continues to resonate with communities around the world several decades later.

THE HEATHEN

The segue into the title track and the penultimate track of the first side, 'The Heathen' is simultaneously hypnotising and slightly frantic, with the repeated vocal hook chanted by Marley and the I Threes in a defiant unison. Swirling synthesisers build throughout, and a fiercely distorted guitar lead from Junior Marvin adds to the overall feeling of resilience in the face of adversity.

EXODUS

The title track and centrepiece of the album is an almost eight-minute-long mini-epic, and an empowering call-to-arms. Marley's rhythmic

Credit: Getty Images

strumming opens 'Exodus', joined gradually by synths and keyboards, a syncopated hi-hat pattern, triumphant horns and nonchalant guitar licks. A slow, almost threatening bass drum thud begins with Marley and the I Three's war-cry "Exodus! Movement of Jah people!" that leads into the main driving beat that kicks in at 40 seconds into the track. Amazingly, all of these elements come together to form a surging and powerful near-perfect composition and innovative mash-up of funk, disco and gospel influences creating a fresh new reggae sound. The lyrics tie together the biblical story of Moses and the Israelites' journey out of exile with the Rastafari hope of being led to freedom by Jah himself, and Marley's own recent self-imposed exile from Jamaica – all delivered with a confident and insistent emphasis on moving forwards with optimism "We know where we're going/We know where we're from/We're leaving Babylon..."

JAMMING

The second side of the record opens up with 'Jamming', and sets the tone for a more laid-back mood from here on out. Breezy and joyful, 'Jamming' is one of the more traditional reggae tracks on the album, and has gone on to become one of Marley's most recognisable songs. Marley casually refers to his recent assassination attempt with lines such as "No bullet can stop us now" and "For life is worth much more than gold", but the track maintains a

ABOVE *(Left to right) Judy Mowatt, Rita Marley and Marcia Griffiths on backing vocals at the Rainbow Theatre in London in June 1977.*

OPPOSITE Exodus *was released just six months after Marley had survived an assassination attempt in Jamaica.*

cheerful atmosphere throughout. It was during the performance of 'Jamming' at the One Love Peace Concert in Jamaica in 1978 that Marley famously joined the hands of rival politicians Edward Seaga and Michael Manley as a gesture of peace.

WAITING IN VAIN

'Waiting in Vain' is an emotive and enchanting song about unreciprocated love. Marley adds a blues rock vibe – including a juicy guitar solo from Junior Marvin – to an otherwise fairly traditional reggae-style track. Rumoured to be about his lover, Cindy Breakspeare (mother of Damian Marley), some say that Rita Marley refused to sing this song along with the rest of the I Threes when The Wailers performed live. The single was one of a few Marley Island singles to feature a non-album B-Side – in this case, the song 'Roots', which was an out-take from the *Rastaman Vibration* sessions.

TURN YOUR LIGHTS DOWN LOW

The theme of romance continues, with 'Turn Your Lights Down Low' introducing a change of pace, ballad-esque keyboards and a sultry repeated refrain from Marley – "I want to give you some love/I want to give you some good, good lovin'" – backed up, as impeccably as ever, by the I Threes. It's the only song from the second side of the record that wasn't released as a single. However, a 1999 remastered version featuring Lauryn Hill achieved commercial success, topping various charts and being nominated for a Grammy Award in 2001.

THREE LITTLE BIRDS

With the singalong chorus of "Singing don't worry about a thing/'Cause every little thing gonna be alright", 'Three Little Birds' radiates with positive energy and reassurance, and is another of Marley's most well-known tunes. There have been different claims as to the source of inspiration for the lyrics. Some say the "Three little birds/Pitch by my doorstep" are the actual three canaries that used to sit on Marley's windowsill in one of his homes in Jamaica; others say it's the I Threes that are the "three little birds" who are "Singing sweet songs/Of melodies pure and true", and some claim Marley is making a biblical reference to The Holy Trinity. Whatever it was, they have resonated with people all around the world for decades, being a particular favourite with children.

ONE LOVE/PEOPLE GET READY

Marley ends the sonic journey of *Exodus* with a dedication to love, Rastafari oneness and the unity of all beings. The ska-style original was recorded by The Wailers and released as a single in Jamaica in 1965. 'One Love/People Get Ready' includes some parts from the 1965 Impressions song, 'People Get Ready', and composition credits on *Exodus* are given to both Marley and Curtis Mayfield. It was released as a single in 1984 as part of the promotion for the greatest hits album, *Legend*. It became a hit, and has been included on most subsequent Marley compilations, as well as on television advertisements for the Jamaica Tourist Board. 'One Love/People Get Ready' is a resolute declaration, celebrating the spiritual strength and extensive inspiration Marley derived from his Rastafari way of life.

> ## "A POLITICAL AND CULTURAL NEXUS
> - TIME MAGAZINE

Credit: Getty Images

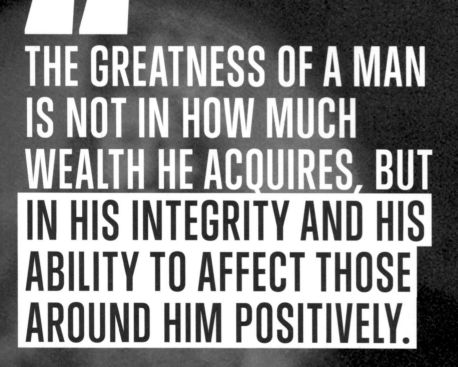

"

THE GREATNESS OF A MAN IS NOT IN HOW MUCH WEALTH HE ACQUIRES, BUT IN HIS INTEGRITY AND HIS ABILITY TO AFFECT THOSE AROUND HIM POSITIVELY.

INSET *The Exodus Tour in 1977 concluded with four shows at London's Rainbow Theatre.*

TITLE:

KAYA

RELEASED:	MARCH 1978	LENGTH:	36:59

A CHILLED OUT AND CHEERFUL RECORD, KAYA ALLOWED MARLEY TO MAKE HIS MESSAGE OF PEACE AND UNITY EVEN MORE ACCESSIBLE

KAYA WAS RECORDED IN THE same sessions as *Exodus*, during Bob Marley and the Wailers' 14-month exile in London following the assassination attempt in 1976. *Exodus* was still in the UK charts when *Kaya* was released – a testament to Marley's popularity and work ethic – and the two are sometimes referred to as sister albums. The feel and sound of *Kaya* is similar to the second side of *Exodus*, with a mainly peaceful and harmonious atmosphere. The name 'Kaya' comes from Jamaican slang for 'dope' (cannabis), and the album's back cover also featured cannabis plants, designed into a 'joint' (a large hand-rolled cigarette filled with cannabis instead of tobacco). Marley received some criticism at the time, with suggestions that he had sold out by not focusing on political or social justice themes, as he often had done on previous records. But beneath the surface of the album that appears to be light-hearted and easy-going, there are still many political and spiritual topics being explored. Keyboards, brass and lead guitar play key roles on

" KAYA WAS ALL DREAMY AND REFLECTIVE.

- UNCUT MAGAZINE

Credit: Getty Images

many tracks on this album, and Marley experiments with some different vocal delivery that contrasts pleasantly with the I Threes' reliably outstanding harmonies. *Kaya* is an album that tends to leave listeners feeling lighter, more relaxed and in no rush to do anything at all.

EASY SKANKING

An ode to Marley's love of smoking cannabis, 'Easy Skanking' was also a musical response to the UK law enforcement who had arrested and charged Marley with possession in June 1977. As the very first verse makes clear ("Excuse me while I light my spliff/ Good God I gotta take a lift"), Marley had not been discouraged from smoking the herb, which was an important part of his Rastafari faith, and something he immensely valued and enjoyed. As Marley repeats frequently throughout the track, 'Easy Skanking' is all about "taking it easy". In 2019, the Marley estate, Island Records and Universal Music Group collaboratively released a new music video for 'Easy

OPPOSITE *Marley performing in front of an image of Haile Selassie, God incarnate for followers of the Rastafarian faith.*

BELOW *A set list written by Bob Marley for The Wailers' Kaya Tour, which took place between May and August 1978.*

Skanking' by Argentinian director Brian Kazez and Pantera Film Studios. It was filmed in Kingston, and features various shots of locals and different aspects of their everyday lives.

KAYA

A remake of a 1971 Wailers single, 'Kaya' is another track dedicated to the love of cannabis. With catchy and repetitive melodic and lyrical hooks, it's a memorable song that makes the listener move along to it. It's hard not to smile as Marley cheerfully declares, "I'm so high, I even touch the sky/Above the falling rain".

IS THIS LOVE

'Is This Love' was the album's biggest hit – peaking at number nine in the UK charts, and at number 12 in Australia. In the years since its release, it has grown in popularity, and is one of Marley's most played songs, having been covered by many other artists and featured in several film soundtracks. It's a mellow Marley take on a universal theme, and with opening lines "I wanna love you, and treat you right/I wanna love you, every day and every night/We'll be together, with a roof right over our heads/We'll share the shelter, of my single bed", it's a wedding playlist favourite. The music video, shot and produced in

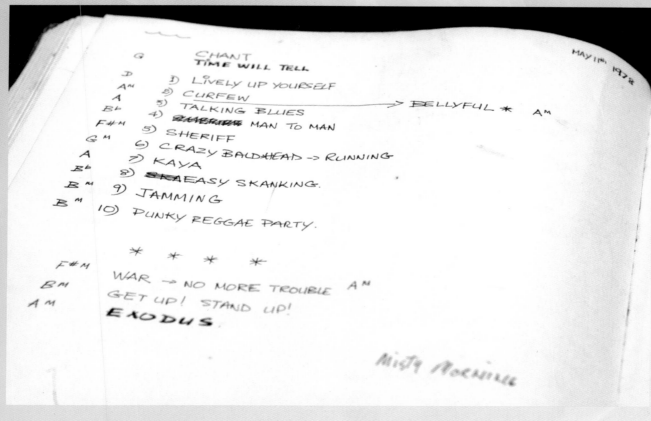

London, features supermodel Naomi Campbell in her first public appearance, at seven years old.

SUN IS SHINING

The first track on the album in a minor key, 'Sun is Shining' has an optimistic outlook, despite the slightly gloomy feel. It's a remake of a track released on a Lee 'Scratch' Perry-produced album (*Soul Revolution*) in 1971. In 1999, 'Sun is Shining' was remixed by Danish house producer Funkstar De Luxe – the first producer the Marley estate allowed to release an official remix. It amplified the lyrical positivity by adding a building repetition to lines such as "I'm a rainbow too", and was an international chart hit, reaching number three in the UK, top ten in several European countries, and number one in Iceland and the US and Canadian dance charts.

SATISFY MY SOUL

The opening lines of 'Satisfy My Soul' – "Oh, please don't rock my boat/'Cause I don't want my boat to be rockin'" – feel like they represent a good general overview of Marley's more easy-going approach to *Kaya*, in comparison to what was done on previous albums. Another re-recording of an old Wailers song, this version carries with it an aura of fulfilment and serenity that is helped along by the cheerful interplay between the horns and piano. The single peaked at number 12 in the UK chart.

SHE'S GONE

The shortest song on the album at just under two and a half minutes, 'She's Gone' is rumoured to be another song inspired by Jamaican model and Damian Marley's mother, Cindy Breakspeare. It's a straightforward love song, given the Marley touch – "Oh, mocking bird, have you ever heard/ Words that I never heard?" – with backing vocals from the I Threes moving effortlessly between high-pitched harmonies, spoken word and sensual whispers.

Credit: Getty Images

MISTY MORNING

'Misty Morning' opens with a dramatic building brass sequence that breaks after 17 seconds, with the introduction of Marley's vocals. This track has some of the most poetic lyrics on the album, including a line that became one of Marley's most famous quotes: "The power of philosophy floats through my head/Light like a feather, heavy as lead".

CRISIS

In 'Crisis', Marley moves easily between vulnerable verses that express his concerns and exasperation at the unjustness of the world ("They say the sun shines for all/But in some people's world, it never shine at all") and confident, hopeful choruses ("No matter what the crisis is/Doing it, doing it doing your thing") that give the whole track a sense of freedom. A heavily syncopated beat and shimmering percussion add that Marley magic.

RUNNING AWAY

'Running Away' sounds at times like Marley is simply talking to himself, and somebody just happened to catch it on record. The vocals are rambling musings that disintegrate into a rough, stream-of-consciousness delivery that sound as if Marley is convincing himself that he did the right thing by leaving Jamaica after the assassination attempt: "I've got to protect my life/And I don't want to live with no strife". The music is fairly simplistic, with repeated melodies evocative of the repeated movement of running. Even the brass solo seems to run away from itself.

TIME WILL TELL

The album closes with an unusual track, featuring elements of folk and blues music. The opening line, "Jah would never give the power to a baldhead" sees Marley, similarly to previous albums, ending with a reminder of his unwavering faith in Jah, and referring to the belief in the eventual fall of 'Babylon' (Western society). Marley warns us in his unique calmly prophetic way that "time will tell" with the simple and sombre refrain, "Think you're in heaven but you're living in hell".

Credit: Getty Images

OPPOSITE *Marley's live shows were full of energy and passion. Here he performs in the Netherlands.*

LEFT *Kaya followed hot on the heels of* Exodus, *and was intended to calm tensions following Marley's shooting in 1976.*

CHAPTER SIX

ROOTS REVOLUTIONARY

ROOTS REVOLUTIONARY

Although Bob Marley's political views were rooted in his Rastafarian ideals, his war against imperialism and oppression resonated across the entire developing world

WORDS BY **HARETH AL BUSTANI**

During Bob Marley's formative years, Jamaica and its capital of Kingston were in a state of dramatic metamorphosis. Despite shaking off the shackles of British colonialism, the country still very much bore the scars of its painful past. As a mixed-race child, Bob had embodied that struggle, ostracised by both sides of his family on racial grounds. Even when he arrived in Kingston as a child, he was subject to abuse, dubbed the "little White boy" or the "little Red boy", and regularly attacked.

Rather than becoming disillusioned, this only furthered his resolve, awakening him to issues of race and colonialism at a young age. It also taught him to seek strength within, as he learned to fight, becoming one of the toughest of the local 'rude boys'. When Marley and The Wailers began their recording career, Jamaica was just beginning to find its footing after four centuries of British colonial rule. Although the country was gripped by nationalistic pride, the disagreements on how best to proceed turned this zealous energy dangerous.

It was also a time of few opportunities. Unemployment was at 35 per cent, and for those in the ghetto of Trench Town, where Bob lived, there seemed to be no escape. The Wailers' first track,

'Simmer Down', was a bold move for a new band in a nascent recording industry. It was a song that spoke from, and to, the anguish of the young rude boys living in Kingston – imploring them not to turn to antisocial behaviour. Even the group's name, The Wailers, was in many ways a political act, reflecting not just the misery of Jamaica's disillusioned youth, but its centuries of colonial anguish.

Yet it was Marley's introduction to Rastafarianism that truly awakened his latent political consciousness. He was given his first grand tour of the faith by Mortimo Planno, a leading Rasta with a vast library of books on Ethiopian history and Black Power. In many ways, Rasta philosophy was inseparable from the politics of the time – rooted in the works of Marcus Garvey, who pioneered notions of Black self-empowerment, Pan-Africanism and the African right of return.

Rastafarians often alluded to the metaphorical 'Babylon', a symbol of Roman Empire, White colonialism, slavery, oppression and destruction, which scattered the African diaspora across the world. It gave Marley a vehicle through which to understand, and direct, his own misfortune, and that of his Trench Town neighbours. He came to understand Jamaica's issues as part of a wider Pan-African Black struggle against a system designed to

oppress it, and in doing so, gradually increased the scope of his political activism.

SLAVE DRIVER

By the late-1960s, Jamaica's ruling right-wing Jamaica Labour Party (JLP) was finding its tight grip slowly pried open by the democratic socialist People's National Party (PNP). When the JLP came to power, among its first acts was to demolish a huge PNP-sympathetic settlement called Back-O-Wall, characterising its large Rasta community as criminals. In its place they built a new community, called Tivoli Gardens, and filled it with JLP supporters. These types of actions had the effect of encouraging factionalism and tribalism, and before long, even Kingston's drug lords and gangs were forced to align themselves with one of the two parties. As ghettos were transformed into 'garrisons', political and gang violence became interwoven, and gunfire became a nightly occurrence.

In the early 1970s, Rastafarians turned to the PNP candidate, Michael Manley, hoping that he might end their persecution, and legalise marijuana. In the 1971-1972 election campaign, Manley travelled across the country, carrying an imperial staff handed to him by Haile Selassie, known as the Rod of Correction, or 'Joshua's Stick'. Bob Marley and the Wailers threw their support behind Manley, touring across the island, performing on the back of a flatbed truck, dubbed the 'PNP Bandwagon'. Manley's island-wide rallies drew huge crowds, worked into an excited frenzy before his appearances by The Wailers, Max Romeo, Delroy Wilson and other musicians. As someone from Nine Mile, a traditional JLP stronghold, Marley's leaning towards the democratic socialist PNP represented the growing shift.

Amidst rising tensions, songs like 'Trench Town Rock' continued to reflect the dire situation of Kingston's impoverished ghettos. Bob implored people not to turn their backs on the slum, portraying the poor as the righteous among society. When Manley rose to power in 1972, the US became paranoid that he might follow in the footsteps of his Caribbean neighbours in Cuba, and began funnelling arms to the JLP. The PNP began arming up in response, and before long, violence spun out of control. Amidst the chaos, Marley was transformed into an international superstar, desperately trying to transcend factional politics.

The Wailers' first album on Island Records featured the powerful call for justice, 'Slave

Credit: Getty Images

Driver'. Drawing on Jamaica's historic role in the international slave trade, he reflects, "Every time I hear the crack of a whip, my blood runs cold". However, he goes a step further, declaring that "Today they say we are free, only to be chained in poverty". In reality, he argues, the enslaved have not been emancipated, but subjected to another form of enslavement, perpetuated by their illiteracy to the machinations of the capitalist system. The song ends on a note of defiance, hinting that the oppressed are beginning to wake up to the reality of their material conditions, and that the slave drivers will soon burn in Hell for their continued sins. He reinforces these ideas in 'Concrete Jungle', where the narrator laments that despite not having physical chains around his feet, he is still bound in the prison of poverty.

BABYLON SYSTEM

Marley's commitment to transnational solidarity was immortalised in 'Get Up, Stand Up', which he co-wrote with Peter Tosh, after seeing the poverty of

Haiti first-hand. The song begins by imploring people to get up and stand up for their rights, and never give up the fight. It urges the downtrodden to ignore preachers, who tell oppressed people to simply accept their fates. Instead, they should rise up, see through the illusion and demand their rights.

However, it was Eric Clapton's cover of Marley's 'I Shot the Sheriff' that catapulted The Wailers to international superstardom. Marley's then-girlfriend, Esther Anderson, claimed the song was an allegory for abortion, where the 'Sheriff' is actually a doctor, prescribing birth control to the singer's lover. However, one of Marley's associates, Lee Jaffe, has a different interpretation – that it was inspired by the police and military jeeps that imposed a curfew on the ghetto, turning it into a virtual "militarised zone". Jaffe saw the song as a metaphor for the righteous revolutionary response to repression. Elaborating, he added, "It made the point that these violent interventions into everyday life in the shantytowns of Jamaica were intrinsically foreign-influenced".

Although the song's narrator admits to shooting a cruel sheriff in self-defence, he denies the charge of killing his deputy. In this manner, the song achieved a remarkable feat; bundling up an exploration of justice, revolution and corruption, beneath the

ABOVE *Marley's music highlighted the issues faced by the world's poor and helped bring them to a wider audience.*

LEFT *The teachings of Jamaican activist Marcus Garvey heavily influenced Bob Marley and his music.*

CHAPTER SIX

facade of a catchy pop song. It's hook "I shot the sheriff" was sung by people of all backgrounds across the planet, transforming Bob Marley and the Wailers into a vehicle for dragging the issues faced by the developing world's downtrodden to the forefront. Marley's music carried these issues from the lips of the poor, to the ears and minds of middle-class intellectuals, uniting them in purpose.

The second half of the 1970s was a chaotic time, as the Cold War continued to manifest itself in proxy wars all across the developing world. With the decline of the British Empire, former colonies in the Middle East desperately tried to find their feet, as both the US and USSR raced to secure access to their oil. Anti-colonial wars were being fought in Africa, and anti-imperial uprisings broke out across South America. Jamaica found itself on the brink of civil war, as the CIA increasingly attempted to destabilise Manley's democratic socialist government.

Despite the dangers, Marley accepted an invitation to perform at the Smile Jamaica Concert, held in an attempt to reconcile the two warring factions – a move that almost led to his death at the hands of an assassin. Shortly before the concert, he told journalist Vivien Goldman, "So much guys have so much – too much – while so many have nothing at all. We don't feel like that is right, because it don't

GET UP, STAND UP
(Marley/Tosh)
From the forthcoming LP "Burnin'"
Produced by Bob Marley and Chris Blackwell
Recorded at Harry J. Studios, Kingston, Jamaica

THE WAILERS

WIP 6167A
WIPX 1268
Tuff Gong Music

℗ 1973 Island Records Ltd

Credit: Alamy

ABOVE *Bob Marley and Peter Tosh wrote 'Get Up, Stand Up' after witnessing the living conditions of Haiti's poor.*

OPPOSITE *"Yeah, me see myself as a revolutionary," Marley once declared during an interview.*

BELOW *Marley's track 'Zimbabwe' inspired the freedom fighters in Rhodesia in their fight for independence in 1980.*

Credit: Getty Images

take a guy a hundred million dollars to keep him satisfied. Everybody have to live."

Among the highlights of the concert was Marley's entrancing performance of 'War', a song he wrote almost entirely using lyrics from Haile Selassie's speech to the UN in 1963: "Until the philosophy which hold one race superior and another inferior is finally and permanently discredited and abandoned, everywhere is war." Like Selassie's speech, it calls for the disintegration of racial and class divisions, and the guarantee of human rights to "all without regard to race". It echoes Selassie's call for the toppling and destruction of the "ignoble and unhappy regimes that hold our brothers in Angola, in Mozambique, and in South Africa in subhuman bondage".

ZIMBABWE

Marley's call for Pan-African liberation and solidarity culminated in his 1977 masterpiece, *Exodus* – encompassing some of his most political work yet, brought to a Biblical scale. Mirroring the flight of the Israelites out of Egypt, the titular track explores the exodus of the Rastafarians away from systems of colonialism and oppression, to "our father's land". Meanwhile, 'So Much Things to Say' draws on the stories of Jesus Christ, Marcus Garvey and the anti-colonial Baptist rebel Paul Bogle, once again equating the political struggle for liberation with rapturous language. Marcus Garvey's ideas resonated strongly with Marley, who remarked, "I and I are the House of David. Our home is Timbuktu, Ethiopia, Africa, where we enjoyed a rich civilisation long

before the coming of the European. Marcus Garvey said that a people without knowledge of their past is like a tree without roots".

In 1978, Marley was presented with a Peace Medal of the Third World by the African delegation to the UN, for his efforts on behalf of disenfranchised Black people across the world. He continued to build on his Pan-African efforts in his 1979 release, *Survival*, which featured another anthem, 'Africa Unite'. Throughout the album Marley highlights class divisions, and the ruling class's obliviousness to "reality", with no care for the people they rule. He describes the system of oppression as a "vampire", and "falling empire", sat atop a ticking "time bomb", asserting that "what goes on up is coming on down".

Although some of his work appeared to mirror a Marxist interpretation of the capitalism and exploitation, as a Rastafarian he considered himself allied not to a system, but to Jah Rastafari. When asked if the Rastas and Prime Minister Manley shared ideologies, he answered, "No mon! Michael Manley is a Marxist-Leninist-Socialist, Rasta is a monarchy. Dig It!" He remained committed to the Ethiopian Solomonic dynasty, even after Haile Selassie's overthrow and death. At a meeting in London, the exiled Ethiopian Crown Prince gave Marley one of Selassie's rings in recognition of his service to Rastafarianism.

Marley's song 'Zimbabwe' became a rallying cry for guerrillas fighting for the liberation of then-Rhodesia. After securing independence, when Zimbabwe raised its flag for the first time, the first words uttered were "Ladies and gentlemen, Bob

Credit: Getty Images

Marley and the Wailers" – introducing the band's performance of 'Zimbabwe'. Bob also headlined a show in Boston, to raise funds for the new country.

Prophetically, the final song on *Uprising* – the last album released during Marley's lifetime – was 'Redemption Song', a pseudo-religious sermon on racial emancipation. He reflects on the atomic energy, and the martyrdom of "our prophets", while drawing on the words of Marcus Garvey, as he declares, "Emancipate yourselves from mental slavery, none but ourselves can free our minds."

In life and death, Bob Marley was elevated to a revolutionary figure at home and beyond. Albert Reid, a Jamaican tractor driver, asserted that if "Bob alone was in power in Jamaica we would have a lovely, peaceful country". Meanwhile, an American Rasta added, "Reggae can make the music much more relevant to the real-life experiences of Black people in America. We listen to our radios more than

ABOVE *While Marley didn't consider himself political, his music railed against oppression and inequality around the world.*

OPPOSITE *Marley was awarded the Peace Medal of the Third World by the United Nations in 1978.*

we read or watch television and what does most of the music say to us? Party, party, dance, dance, get down, get down. But a reggae song might deal with the lack of food for the people, or about the war in Zimbabwe, or the need for Blacks to unite. That's why it's so important for our people to hear reggae."

Reflecting on Marley's legacy, former Wailer Judy Mowatt said his political views were simple enough for people of different languages and cultures to understand: "He sang about the need for love and unity amongst all people." Marley himself believed the secret to his universality was his refusal to compromise: "I'm one of dem tough ones".

SURVIVAL

RELEASED:	OCTOBER 1979	LENGTH:	38:02

SURVIVAL IS THE MOST POLITICAL OF MARLEY'S ALBUMS, AN URGENT CALL TO PAN-AFRICAN UNITY AND A PAEAN TO BLACK SURVIVAL IN THE FACE OF OPPRESSION

WHEN *SURVIVAL* WAS BEING RECORDED, Bob Marley was already ill with the cancer that would kill him within a year and a half. Although Marley did not yet know how serious his condition was, there is an urgency to the album that is in marked contrast to the relaxed, love-soaked vibe of 1978's *Kaya*. The first in what was planned as a trilogy of albums, *Survival* was originally entitled 'Black Survival', indicating the Pan-Africanist themes of many of the songs. It was also the only one of Bob Marley's studio albums not to be produced by Chris Blackwell, the production duties being taken by Alex Sadkin, a Blackwell protégé who was head engineer at Island Records' Compass Point Studio in Nassau. The change in producer made for a less polished, more Jamaican sound to the record, possibly contributing to its lack of hit singles. The cover, designed by Neville Garrick, featured 48 African flags (15 no longer in use) as well as the flag of Papua New Guinea. Note the black-and-white strip that is the

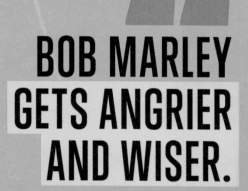

" BOB MARLEY GETS ANGRIER AND WISER.

- MELODY MAKER

Credit: Getty Images

background to the title: it's the layout for carrying African slaves on a slave ship.

SO MUCH TROUBLE IN THE WORLD

"A likkle more drums." That's what Marley says at the start. Then, the song cuts in and immediately we hear that we're in a different place, with Marley singing in an understated vein, pointing to the world's troubles rather than himself as performer and star. It bears comparison with 'Soul Rebel' musically, then goes into a funky bridge, modulating from the minor chords (A minor, D minor and E minor) of verse and chorus to G9 and F9 chords when Marley and the I Threes swap lines from "So you think you've found the solution". The Barrett brothers provide the rocksteady drum and bass backing, while Junior Marvin takes care of the restrained guitar.

ZIMBABWE

Rhodesia became Zimbabwe on 18 April 1980, ending White rule, and Bob Marley sang 'Zimbabwe' at the celebration held to mark the event, paying passage for himself and The Wailers. Indeed, "Every man got the right to decide his own destiny" were the very first words sung after the official flag raising to mark the birth of the new country. But since the

ABOVE *Bob Marley and the Wailers performed a free concert for 100,000 Zimbabweans the day after the official independence celebration.*

LEFT *Marley at his home at 56 Hope Road, where he experienced an assassination attempt.*

official celebration was closed to the public, Marley played a free concert the next day for an audience of 100,000 Zimbabweans. Marley was the only non-Zimbabwean act to appear at the celebration. It was fitting. His music was part of the soundtrack for Zimbabwean guerrillas during the Chimurenga ('uprising' in Shona), the long struggle for independence. Now, he was there for its apotheosis.

TOP RANKIN'

In the late 1970s, Jamaica was in a mess. Political and economic instability had created a violent mixture and the country's politicians were not above using this to settle scores and intimidate and kill opponents. For a man as dedicated to unity as Bob Marley, this came as an almost personal wound. Determined not to be drawn into factional politics, Marley used a classic reggae phrase as the hook in this song appealing for the people to unite in the face of the politicians' attempts to divide them into warring parties and set them at each other's throats. The brass section, prominent on this track, consisted of trombone and trumpet.

BABYLON SYSTEM

"Babylon system is the vampire." For Bob Marley, Babylon resonated as the synonym for oppression and corruption. With its roots in the forced exile of the Jewish people to Babylon, the concept was borrowed by the descendants of slaves who had themselves been taken into involuntary exile on slave ships crossing the Atlantic. But the syncopated, gospel feel to the track shows that while Babylon might be a vampire, sucking blood from suffering people worldwide, the recognition of what lies behind the mask removes much of its power. It's time to tell the children the truth about the world they live in so that they too can sing its demise, to replace it with something better.

SURVIVAL

Yes, it does sound like 'Exodus'. It also comes as the last track on the first side of the vinyl album. While 'Survival' does not match the extraordinary intensity of 'Exodus', which was written in the immediate aftermath of the assassination attempt on Marley, it serves as a hymn to the extraordinary toughness of the Black people who had survived the crucible of slavery and the ongoing horrors of the dark age of modern technology harnessed by the forces of Babylon. The Shadrach, Meshach and Abednego of the song were Jewish youths who refused to bow before the graven image of the king of Babylon and, in punishment, were thrown into a fiery pit. But God preserved them from the flames.

AFRICA UNITE

'Africa Unite' is a full-throated expression of Marley's Pan-African allegiance combined with the deep, personal appropriation of the story of the Babylonian exile of the Jews as symbol and prefiguration for the exile and, in Marley's case, hoped-for return of Black

people to the promised land: Africa. With its theme of return to the Promised Land, it borrows a couplet, almost word for word, from 'Exodus', setting the lyrics against a stripped-down reggae beat enlivened with a rather unexpected flute motif winding through the song. As no flute player is credited among the musicians on *Survival*, it's likely that the 'flute' was played on the synthesiser by Earl 'Wire' Lindo, The Wailers' keyboard player.

ONE DROP

The characteristic rhythmic pattern of reggae music is the 'one drop' drum pattern and, rather helpfully, this song, a paean to the beat and reggae unity, demonstrates it beautifully. Carlton Barrett, the drumming half of the sibling rhythm section that underpinned The Wailers' sound, was the master of this rhythm. A typical rock drum pattern has the bass drum playing on the first beat of the bar and the snare drum on the third beat. The 'one drop' rhythm omits the first beat (dropping the one) and plays the snare and bass drums on the third beat of the four-beat bar, creating a false offbeat effect that adds to the overall offbeat rhythms characteristic of reggae.

BELOW *Although it didn't spawn hit singles,* Survival *still sold enough copies for The Wailers to be awarded a gold record.*

OPPOSITE *The attempt on Marley's life left more of an impression on him than just the bullet holes in his wall.*

Credit: Getty Images

Credit: Getty Images

RIDE NATTY RIDE

The harmonica part on 'Ride Natty Ride' is played by the most unlikely of all The Wailers: Lee Jaffe. A New York City Jew, Jaffe had moved to Brazil in the late 1960s, making experimental films before returning to New York and the avant-garde art scene. Jaffe knew where to get the best weed in New York, so it is perhaps not surprising that when Marley was in town and they met at the premiere of *Last Tango in Paris*, the two men hit it off. Jaffe went to Jamaica on holiday and ended up staying for five years, sharing Marley's house when the singer moved to 56 Hope Road, Kingston (now the site of the Bob Marley Museum) and playing harmonica in jam and recording sessions with Bob Marley and the Wailers. Jaffe, a man with some very useful connections, became The Wailers' fix-it guy, sorting out anything from booking venues to finding weed. And playing the harmonica.

AMBUSH IN THE NIGHT

On 3 December 1976, seven armed men broke into Marley's house, where The Wailers were taking a break from rehearsing. Rita Marley, sitting in her car in the drive, was shot in the head. Bob Marley was shot in the chest and arm. Two other men at the house were also shot. But nobody was killed. The attempted assassination was probably due to Marley agreeing to play in a Jamaican unity concert that had been drawn into the dispute between the two main political factions in the country. Marley went ahead with the concert two days later, then wrote this song against the powerful men who would keep people ignorant and manipulable.

WAKE UP AND LIVE

A fitting song to follow 'Ambush in the Night' and Marley's brush with violent death. The horn-driven riff, with a funky saxophone solo by Glen DaCosta, exhorts people to 'Wake Up and Live' because, as Marley now knew only too well, it was better to "live big today; tomorrow you buried in a casket". The track was co-written by Anthony 'Sangie' Davis, with key lyrics inspired by a drive Marley and Davis took together when detours and potholes inspired Davis to say, "Life is one big road with a lot of signs, so when you riding through the ruts, don't complicate your mind". Later, when he spotted a billboard (for Andrew's antacid of all things) proclaiming 'Wake up and live,' Davis had the chorus too.

MARLEY WAS SHOT IN THE CHEST AND ARM.

"
TRUE FRIENDS ARE LIKE STARS; YOU CAN ONLY RECOGNISE THEM WHEN IT'S DARK AROUND YOU.

Bob Marley, The Wailers and the I Threes on the road in 1978.

Credit: Getty Images

TITLE:

UPRISING

RELEASED:	JUNE 1980	LENGTH:	35:53

ON THE COVER, BOB MARLEY RAISES HIS ARMS TO GOD. UPRISING IS, FIRST AND FOREMOST, A HYMN TO THE SOURCE OF MARLEY'S INSPIRATION

THE SONGS ON THE *UPRISING* album were recorded in the same burst of creativity that produced *Survival*. But where *Survival* is a paean to Pan-African unity and the survival of African people in the face of the forced diaspora of slavery, *Uprising* is an extended hymn to God. Almost all the songs on the album are addressed to Jah or reflect on the tensions between sacred and secular, tensions felt keenly by Marley in his combined role as prophet of Rastafarianism and global superstar. When Marley presented the first version of the album to Chris Blackwell, Island Records' director and Marley's long-time producer, Blackwell gently suggested adding a couple more up-tempo numbers to alleviate the generally quite sombre feel to the record. Revealing the pragmatism with which Marley combined the roles of prophet and star, he came back with the jaunty skank of 'Coming in from the Cold' and the inimitable reggae groove of 'Could You Be Loved', the album's hit single. But it's the final track, 'Redemption Song', that serves as Marley's epitaph. Less than a year after the release of *Uprising*, Marley would be dead.

Credit: Alamy

REAL SITUATION

A strangely jaunty song about the end of the world, 'Real Situation' shows Marley as prophet of the apocalypse. But rather than wrap himself in sackcloth and ashes, calling the people to repentance, in this song Marley accepts the incorrigibility of the powers of this world, who are the representatives of the Babylon system he excoriated in *Survival*, and views the coming reckoning as a necessary consequence of the sinfulness of the rulers of nations. In the face of this inevitability, the oddly joyous lilt to the song comes into focus: what cannot be avoided must be accepted, but it is even better to embrace it.

BAD CARD

'Bad Card' is one of the few tracks on the album to address, reputedly, Marley's more personal concerns, to wit, his dispute with his now ex-manager, Don Taylor. A larger-than-life character, Taylor had hustled his way from the streets of Kingston to the US, learning the deal-making behind showbusiness while managing Little Anthony and the Imperials during stints playing Las Vegas. Taylor met Marley when organising a concert in 1973. A year later, he turned up on Marley's doorstep. The pair talked, and shook hands on the deal: Taylor became Marley's manager. He negotiated the deal with Island Records that set Marley on the way to international stardom, and took one of the bullets meant for the singer in the assassination attempt on 3 December 1976. But the pair fell out when Marley accused Taylor of fraud. According to Taylor, Marley emphasised the end of their agreement by brandishing a gun at him. Even so, Taylor oversaw Marley's funeral arrangements, but then inevitably became involved in the long dispute over Marley's estate.

WE AND DEM

Another stripped-down skank with minimal accompaniment, 'We and Dem' is a further jeremiad against the Babylon system and a prophetic statement of the necessity for a just accounting. After all, it's what the Bible says, and Marley, who knew the scriptures well, was aware that the story of Israel was the story of a people that had no friends among the powerful of this world. But with men losing their faith, there seems little hope of a resolution in this fallen world; only Jah can make things right.

COMING IN FROM THE COLD

The cover of *Uprising* shows Marley, arms uplifted and dreads flowing, rising into the sunrise, a young, Black god. But on the back cover, a photo of Marley and The Wailers, Bob looks tired and thin, older than his 35 years. Although Marley did not know of the cancer attacking his body during the recording of *Uprising*, some lyrics suggest that a deeper knowledge had found its way into his soul. For those who would all too shortly be mourning him, the lines, "Why do you look so sad and forsaken/When one door is closed, don't you know another is open", seem to be written both as farewell and reassurance.

ABOVE Uprising *would be Bob Marley's last release in his lifetime, as less than a year later he was dead.*

LEFT *Bob Marley and the Wailers perform at the Crystal Palace Bowl in London on 7 June 1980.*

SUCH A TOUR DE FORCE IS AS MOVING AS IT IS DEEPLY TROUBLING.

- ROLLING STONE

WORK

The most rhythmical of the tracks on side one of *Uprising*, 'Work' is an upbeat account of the necessity and burden of exactly what the title says. For a reputedly laid-back Rastaman, Bob Marley had an extraordinary work ethic, inspired in part by a sense of his duty to Jah. In the seven years since signing for Island Records, Marley had recorded eight studio and two live albums, at least three of them all-time classics, as well as touring incessantly. So while the image of the marijuana smoker is one of a dude too blissed out to do anything, Marley was the opposite: the herb, an entry point into deeper communion with God, fired him to preach the message he perceived in his relationship with Jah.

ZION TRAIN

If the apocalyptic lyrics of 'Real Situation' bear witness to one facet of Marley's prophetic voice, the joyous rapture of 'Zion Train' highlights the other side of it. For the corollary of the apocalypse is salvation for God's chosen people and a return to their Promised Land. The solid bass and drums underlie the message, their solidity making the prophecy more real: with such a foundation how could the train not fail to arrive? The very word 'Zion' carries so many layers of meaning in this song as to be almost inexhaustible, from Promised Land through lost Eden to the new Jerusalem: it's a very physical idea of heaven that sits well with Marley's visceral take on spirituality. This is a religion of the guts, as well as the heart and the soul.

PIMPER'S PARADISE

'Pimper's Paradise' is an unusual song both in the context of the religious concerns of *Uprising* and the wider field of Marley's work, as he rarely sang about women other than to praise or declare love. 'Pimper's Paradise' is a warning against becoming trapped in the sort of lifestyle and mindset that might end

INSET *Uprising is thought to be one of Marley's most spiritual albums.*

Credit: Getty Images

INSET *Marley meeting a fan in Toulon, France, on 30 June 1980.*

with a woman having so lost her sense of self that she ends up working for a pimp. Even so, Marley's sympathies remain with the victim of the pimps.

COULD YOU BE LOVED

From the very first bar of the syncopated, palm-muted guitar riff that begins 'Could You Be Loved', you think you are listening to a hit. Then the rhythm section kicks in, and Bob starts singing the title, and you know you are listening to the last great dance classic from The Wailers. There's a suggestion that the tempo was increased slightly in production, but if so, that shows Chris Blackwell's unerring ear for rhythms: the song became a staple in 1980s' clubs, played from Kingston to London to the Mediterranean. 'Could You Be Loved' was a huge hit in the UK, reaching number five in the charts, certified platinum and selling over 600,000 copies.

The interplay between the guitar groove and the rhythm section takes the song as far from traditional reggae as Marley ever went, as did his experimentation with exotic instruments: that sound that comes in sounding like the breath of an asthmatic saw in the second bar is actually a Brazilian cuica, a friction drum that is played by rubbing a wet cloth up and down a stick stuck on the underside of the drum skin inside the body of the drum. Yes, you have read that correctly.

FOREVER LOVING JAH

The album settles back into a laid-back skank, the assurance as present in the lyric of love and salvation in the love of God as it is in The Wailers' rhythm section. 'Forever Loving Jah' was written not long after the attempted assassination of Marley while he was in temporary exile from Jamaica, but it rests in the surety of Marley's belief and praise of his creator, whatever trials and burdens are laid upon him. The song weaves biblical quotations seamlessly into Marley's own thoughts, showing the deep union between the two: Marley thought and sang in biblical metaphors for, as he says, paraphrasing the Bible, God's wisdom is hidden from the wise, but made manifest to children and babes.

REDEMPTION SONG

The final track on the last album released in Marley's lifetime has become the man's epitaph, and never has a popular music star penned such a self obituary. 'Redemption Song' is just Bob Marley and a guitar, the accompaniment so sparse as to leave reggae behind and reach a sort of universal musical language reaching out to anyone who has ears to hear. Having identified himself with reggae, Marley goes beyond a particular musical form to highlight the message behind his music: redemption. Redemption as freedom, freedom in redemption, and Marley identifies himself and his music with both. He is the music and the music is redemption. No deeper or more profound statement of music and its power to affect and transform the player and the listener could ever be made, and it provides an apt epitaph to Bob Marley's journey into the heart of music.

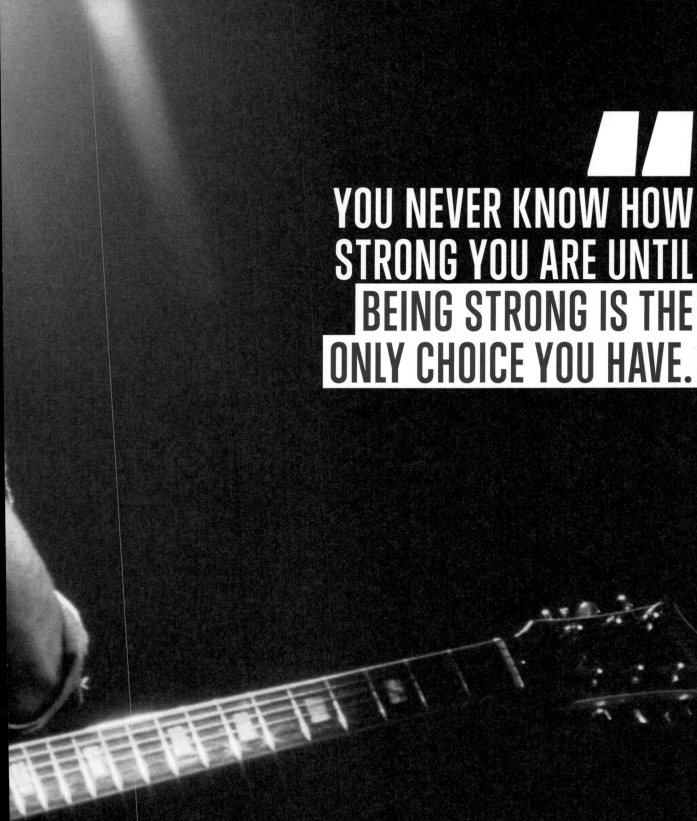

"
YOU NEVER KNOW HOW
STRONG YOU ARE UNTIL
BEING STRONG IS THE
ONLY CHOICE YOU HAVE.

TITLE:

CONFRONTATION

RELEASED:	MAY 1983	LENGTH:	37:47

THE POSTHUMOUSLY RELEASED CONFRONTATION, STITCHED TOGETHER FROM OUTTAKES AND DEMOS, PROVES A SURPRISINGLY WORTHY EPITAPH TO BOB MARLEY'S CAREER

ISLAND RECORDS' CHRIS BLACKWELL AND The Wailers worked hard in the two years after Marley's death to produce a final record worthy of his legacy. While *Confrontation* is inevitably somewhat patchy, it remains a worthy coda to Marley's all-too-short life. Working from demos, Blackwell and The Wailers added vocals from the I Threes to some of the songs, removing the original backing tracks by The Meditations to obtain a uniform sound throughout. The cover, designed by Neville Garrick, shows Marley as St George, slaying the dragon that is Babylon. Not coincidentally, St George is also the patron saint of Ethiopia, and the inside cover has a remarkable painting, in the style of Ethiopian iconography, depicting the victory of Ethiopian forces over the invading Italian army at the Battle of Adwa on 1 March 1896. The Ethiopian victory ensured that Ethiopia would remain independent, uncolonised by European powers, until its brief annexation by Mussolini's forces in 1937.

CHANT DOWN BABYLON

'Chant Down Babylon' was first recorded during the sessions that produced the *Uprising* album. Chant is a Rastafarian tradition, combining voices with drums and percussion, and the meditation-inducing qualities of marijuana to produce an experience of unity with the community, the earth and God. The song also highlights Marley's belief that music, and in particular his music, was a vehicle for spiritual powers able to confront and destroy Babylon. The song though is less chant than a 'one drop' reggae rhythm. Unusually, the drums on this track are played by Carlton 'Santa' Davis rather than The Wailers' usual drummer, Carlton Barrett.

BUFFALO SOLDIER

From the opening blare of brass, 'Buffalo Soldier' is immediately recognisable. The biggest hit from *Confrontation*, the upbeat skank tells a story that,

until Marley highlighted it, was largely unknown. The Buffalo Soldiers were Black Americans who served in the US Army, many fighting in the Indian Wars of the 19th century after the end of the American Civil War. Marley makes them into a symbol of the wider Black struggle and the particular struggle faced by Rastafarians to live out their faith in the face of a determinedly secular and

Credit: Wikimedia Commons

irreligious society. The song reached number four in the UK singles charts.

JUMP NYABINGHI

First recorded during the *Kaya* sessions, 'Jump Nyabinghi' is another jaunty celebration of Rastafarian unity, a unity reinforced by dance and, of course, the herb referenced in the lyrics. 'Nyabinghi' comes from the name of an African tribe, but Marley uses it to refer to Rastafarians in the song. With its lyric of collective dance, Marley also sees the connection with the biblical story of Joshua bringing down the walls of Jericho by leading the Israelites in procession around the city with their horns blaring. As music and movement brought down the walls of Jericho, so it will also bring down Babylon.

MIX UP, MIX UP

'Mix Up, Mix Up' is one of the older songs on the album, dating from the *Kaya* sessions or even before. Marley's vocals sound notably different on this recording; full-throated and experimental, a man still in the prime of health and strength. The song

" A VALUABLE, WELCOME DOCUMENT.

- ROLLING STONE

stretches into a long reggae groove with the vocals from the I Threes and unusual synthesiser strings. Marley here proclaims his allegiance to his roots in the Jamaican countryside, asserting that neither

INSET *The Buffalo Soldiers were Black US cavalry regiments who fought during the Indian Wars.*

fame nor riches have changed him from the man he was made by his upbringing.

GIVE THANKS AND PRAISES

There's no doubt to who Marley would give thanks and praise: God was the axle around which his worldview turned, and praise and worship was a major – possibly *the* major – element of his song writing. 'Give Thanks and Praises' features a particularly laid-back accompaniment from The Wailers, although the brass section injects some urgency to the song. The I Threes all but whisper their accompaniment. The reference to Ham as the ancestor of the prophet among the sons of Noah refers to the belief among some people that the descendants of Ham were the Black people, although that is stated nowhere in the passage in Genesis.

BLACKMAN REDEMPTION

'Blackman Redemption' was released as a single in 1978 before being collected into *Confrontation*. The song was produced by Lee 'Scratch' Perry. Another version of the song exists, released as a sound system dub plate on acetate, that sounds more like a Perry production. The song examines biblical history and places the prophets of Rastafarianism, in particular the Emperor Haile Selassie, in the line of succession from the kings of Israel, David and Solomon, as the Ethiopian kings claim descent in direct line from King Solomon and the Queen of Sheba.

TRENCH TOWN

The warm brass that opens 'Trench Town', followed swiftly by the I Threes' chorus, all lead into Marley's appreciation of Trench Town. Kingston 12, as it is also known, was his old stamping ground in the Jamaican capital. Trench Town produced many ska, rocksteady and reggae musicians, most obviously Marley himself, who spent much of his youth knocking around First Street. It was a notoriously tough and violent part of Kingston, home to a gang warfare epidemic. 56 Hope Road, Marley's house and now the Marley Museum in Kingston, lies about four kilometres northeast of Trench Town.

STIFF NECKED FOOLS

Bob Marley recorded the original demo of 'Stiff Necked Fools' with two young Jamaican musicians, Cleveland 'Clevie' Browne (drums) and Wycliffe 'Steely' Johnson (keyboards). The Marley demo was the first time that Steely and Clevie worked together, but it would not be the last. They would prove one of Marley's most enduring and influential legacies within the Kingston music scene. Steely introduced drum machines into reggae studio recordings, while

as a duo they produced a huge number of 12-inch and dub singles that provided the template for dancehall and then ragga. Dancehall later found its way into mainstream Western pop music through mega-selling acts, such as Drake and Sean Paul.

I KNOW

Another experimental track Marley left unfinished, 'I Know' sounds different to most of his later work, harking back to Marley's R&B roots, with the I Threes sounding more like The Supremes than Bob's backing singers. The rhythm is also different from the normal 'one drop' drum pattern, although it's not certain if the synthesised keyboards swirling on top of the beat were added in production following Marley's death. Lyrically, the song is in praise of God, and offers reassurance that He will be waiting at the other side of the afflictions of this life.

RASTAMAN LIVE UP

An exhortation to endurance and survival – suggesting that the track was originally laid down during the *Survival* sessions – 'Rastaman Live Up' was first released as a single in 1978, produced by Lee 'Scratch' Perry. The version on *Confrontation* differs from the Perry version, with a longer lyric and re-recorded rhythm track. The song conflates African tribes, Rastafarians and David and Samson, the great giant-slaying heroes of the Bible, as symbols of courage and not giving up.

BELOW *Bob Marley with the I Threes at the Crystal Palace Bowl in 1980; his last and biggest show in London.*

RIGHT *Confrontation was compiled using demos and outtakes recorded during previous studio sessions.*

Credit: Getty Images

CHAPTER SEVEN

LIVE
FOREVER

LIVE FOREVER

Bob Marley was the first Third World superstar but now he sought to establish himself in Africa among the people he regarded as his own

WORDS BY **EDOARDO ALBERT**

By the late-1970s, Bob Marley was the uncrowned king of Jamaica. When he was not away touring, people gravitated to his home at 56 Hope Road. There all manner of characters would gather, from ghetto youth through gangsters and dealers to ranting schizophrenics. Fishermen might drop off a catch, farmers leave crops of fruit to be juiced. And, more than anything else, people just hung out on the front steps under the awning or played football. Come the cool of evening, Marley would often go round to the back of the house with a guitar and spend the evening with his closest friends, playing music old and new and smoking into the night. It was a good life.

But it was not all just hanging out. In July 1979, Marley and The Wailers headlined the second Reggae Sunsplash Festival. He had missed the first, in the previous year, as The Wailers were touring, but Marley was determined to help boost the festival and the lift it gave to Jamaica as a whole – with Marley as its visible face, the country was turning into a major tourist destination. When The Wailers played Reggae Sunsplash II there were as many Europeans and Americans in the audience as Jamaicans. But the weather gods turned the event from a sunsplash into a water splash, dousing crowd and stage in tropical volumes of rain. By this time, though, The Wailers were such experienced musicians that they took the conditions in their stride, turning the wet and muddy stage floor to their advantage by sliding all over it.

In October, Bob Marley and the Wailers set out on a long tour to promote the new *Survival* album. The schedule was tough, but at least the US part would be over before winter really kicked in; The Wailers, like migrating birds, were heading south with the sun, rounding off the tour in Trinidad and Tobago, and the Bahamas before finishing with their very first concert in the mother continent: Gabon in Africa. The tour began with a show at Harvard University before a concert at Madison Square Garden and then seven concerts (in just four days) at the legendary Apollo Theater in Harlem, New York. Marley himself had asked for the Apollo Theater residency. He was conscious that, so far, his music had spread far more widely among White people in America than among Black Americans. Black music radio stations generally avoided playing reggae and even after the Harlem shows, Marley struggled to get a hearing for his music from Black Americans.

Having played a concert in Dallas, Texas, on 7 December, The Wailers flew to Trinidad for concerts on 8 and 9 December. However, the organisation was poor and when fans without tickets burst into the stadium the police fired tear gas into the crowd. Further shows in the southern states of America followed before a final show in Nassau, Bahamas on 15 December. It had been a gruelling tour. Rather than return to Jamaica, Marley flew to Florida to stay with his mother for a while. Jamaica was in a feverish state, with rivalry between the two main political parties intense and often bloody. Elections were scheduled for 30 October 1980 but levels of violence were already rising by the end of 1979. For Marley, home was becoming a dangerous place.

Marley and The Wailers started 1980 on a plane, crossing the Atlantic. But this time, they touched down in Gabon, West Africa. They had been invited to play in the capital, Libreville, and Marley, delighted at being asked to play on African soil for the first time, had been willing to play for free. However, Don Taylor, his manager, insisted that they keep the $40,000 they were offered in order to cover The Wailers' costs. The shows themselves were not what Marley had hoped. A child of the poor countryside and the poorer ghetto, he found himself playing to the Gabonese elite rather than the people. However, the tour would have wider repercussions. Just before leaving Gabon, Marley discovered that the Gabonese government had paid Taylor $60,000 for the shows. During an intense confrontation with Taylor, Marley found out that his manager had been regularly creaming off the top of his earnings.

Returning to his mother's house in Florida, Marley met with his old manager, Danny Sims, and decided that he should take over running the band's career. But to do so, Taylor had to agree to close the contract he had with Marley. The negotiations were brutal. Calling Taylor to visit him, Marley, with his friend Allan 'Skill' Cole, forced Taylor to the ground and threatened to shoot him with the guns they were brandishing. It took the intervention of Marley's mother and his son, Ziggy, to save Taylor.

In southern Africa, the long struggle for emancipation had reached its climax in one of the apartheid states: on 17 April 1980, Rhodesia was set to become Zimbabwe, ending White minority rule and ushering in a new government led by Robert Mugabe. For Marley, it was a privilege and honour to be invited to play at the festivities arranged to mark the birth of this new nation, so much so that he personally paid the £100,000 it cost to transport The Wailers and their entourage to Zimbabwe for the independence day ceremony. But as Marley stood on

RIGHT *Bob Marley in New York in October 1979 during the US leg of The Wailers' Survival Tour.*

Credit: Getty Images

stage, he saw this dream of freedom turning into a nightmare before his eyes. The concert was attended by international dignitaries and the functionaries of the new ruling ZANU political party that was Mugabe's power base. Excluded and standing outside were ordinary Zimbabweans and the fighters of the other main group of guerrillas, Joshua Nkomo's ZAPU. As The Wailers struck up, the ZAPU men and women forced their way into the stadium. In response, the police and ZANU fighters inside started striking out with rifle butts and batons, charging into protesters in the same manner that the soldiers and police of the old Rhodesian state

had done. With the celebrations dissolving into chaos, the police started firing off tear gas. In the end, a soldier came out on stage, put a water-soaked cloth over Marley's face, and led him backstage. The I Threes went back to their hotel but, switching on the TV, they saw that the rest of The Wailers had resumed the concert so they rushed back, only to arrive as the band were coming off stage. To make up for the chaos and violence of the first show, The Wailers played a free concert the next day to an audience of a hundred thousand Black Africans.

Before flying to Africa for the Zimbabwean independence day celebration, Marley had been in

MY MUSIC WILL GO ON FOREVER. MAYBE IT'S A FOOL SAY THAT, BUT... MY MUSIC WILL GO ON FOREVER.

- BOB MARLEY ON HIS MUSICAL LEGACY

the studio recording tracks for *Uprising*, the last album to be released during his lifetime. The album was released on 10 June 1980 and the promotional tour kicked off 11 days beforehand with a show in Switzerland. It was a huge tour, highlighting Marley's popularity in Europe: he played to over a million fans in 12 countries between 30 May and 23 September. It would be the last tour he would ever make.

Perhaps the tour's highlight was the show at the San Siro stadium in Milan, Italy. A hundred thousand Italians came to see the prophet of Rastafarianism play in the country that had briefly annexed Ethiopia in the 1930s, deposing Emperor Haile Selassie for the first time. The London show at the Crystal Palace Bowl had the band playing on the stage behind a lake. To get closer to The Wailers the crowd spilled into the lake: it was a wild, wet show.

When the European leg of the tour ended in July, The Wailers headed back to Jamaica to rest before the American half of the tour began in September. But with elections nearing in his homeland, it was too dangerous for Marley to go home. He headed to New York where he visited the bar that was the de facto base of Paul Castellano, the Mafia godfather. Castellano's son was a fan and the Mafia boss was thinking of investing in Marley: America remained a market that The Wailers had not fully cracked. With

OPPOSITE *Many of Bob Marley's children have followed in their father's footsteps, going on to enjoy successful music careers.*

BELOW *Around 100,000 fans turned up to see Bob Marley and the Wailers at the San Siro in Milan, Italy, in June 1980.*

his Island Records' contract soon to expire, Marley was thinking of moving elsewhere. But other events would soon make all this moot.

The Wailers kicked off their American tour in Boston on 14 September before moving to New York. Unusually, Marley had arranged to stay in a different hotel from The Wailers. After two shows opening for The Commodores at Madison Square Garden, Marley went for a run in Central Park. He collapsed. His companions helped him back to his hotel but Marley was clearly seriously ill. The Wailers, staying at a different hotel, were not initially told about Marley's illness. After spending Sunday in hospital undergoing tests, Marley went to see Chris Blackwell, who was staying in New York, on Monday morning to tell him that he had inoperable cancer. The doctors gave Marley just three weeks to live.

Wary of any implied condescension, Blackwell did not have any photos of himself and Marley. Before leaving, Marley insisted they have their picture taken together. Then Marley left. He was heading for

Pittsburgh where The Wailers were waiting for him. Knowing he was dying, he intended to play a final show. It took place on 23 September at the Stanley Theater. Reaching deep into himself, Marley played a 90-minute set and a succession of encores.

The rest of the tour was cancelled. The Wailers returned to Jamaica, leaving Marley in New York with Rita Marley. Then comes one of the most mysterious episodes of Marley's life. With the doctors giving him only weeks to live, Marley sought out Archbishop Abuna Yesehaq, a primate of the Ethiopian Orthodox Church whom Haile Selassie had sent to the Americas to minister to Rastafarians and expatriate Ethiopians. The Ethiopian Orthodox Church is one of the oldest Christian churches in the world. Rita had been baptised into the church in 1972. Now, dying, Marley sought baptism too and the Archbishop received him into the church in the presence of his wife and some of his children. Marley then flew to Germany where a Dr Issels provided unorthodox treatments to terminal cancer patients. At first, the regime helped, but by May of 1981 Marley's health was failing and he determined to return home. But on the flight to Miami, his health deteriorated and on landing he was taken to Cedars of Lebanon Hospital. Bob Marley died there on 11

May 1981. His state funeral in Jamaica took place on 21 May. Afterwards, his body was taken back to Nine Mile where he was buried with his guitar.

Marley had died intestate and, not surprisingly, his death started a period of legal wrangling over the proceeds. In the end, Chris Blackwell bought the whole estate from the Jamaican government, paying $8.6 million for it, before signing over the income from the estate to Marley's children. The final studio album from Bob Marley and the Wailers, *Confrontation*, was released in May 1983, the record put together from other recordings made during the *Survival* and *Uprising* sessions and demos developed into full songs. Then, in May 1984, Island released the compilation album, *Legend*. The Wailers had been primarily a live band; their records sold well but not spectacularly. *Legend* changed all that. If there is one reggae album people own, it's *Legend*. It sold over 20 million copies and cemented the Bob Marley legend.

While no one else could have Bob Marley's global impact, many of his children followed in his musical footsteps. The first to achieve success was his son with Rita, Ziggy, whose band, the Melody Makers, also featured his siblings Sharon, Cedella and Stephen. Ziggy's voice was similar to that of his father and Melody Makers' shows featured much of Bob Marley's original songs as well as their own. Ziggy has gone on to a successful solo career as has his younger brother, Stephen. Marley's youngest son, Damian, born to Cindy Breakspeare, has also had a successful musical career, winning four Grammys.

As with his music, the Marley image continues to cast its spell worldwide. What he would have made of its use as a marketing tool to sell Jamaica as a tourist destination is another matter; it seems at odds with the fierceness of much of his message. But while the revolutionary Marley might baulk at his commercialisation, the businessman would probably have approved: at the least, it has ensured the prosperity of his extended and growing family.

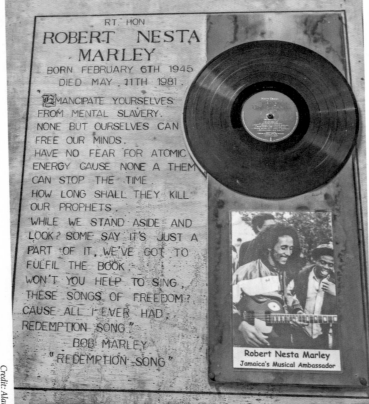

Credit: Alamy

LEFT *A memorial to Marley quoting the lyrics to 'Redemption Song'.*

OPPOSITE *Bob Marley relaxing at 56 Hope Road in 1979.*

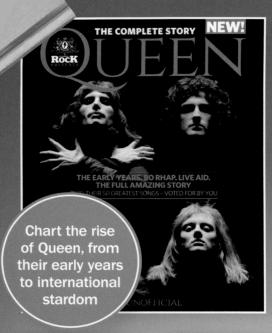

THE COMPLETE STORY **NEW!**

Rock PRESENTS

QUEEN

THE EARLY YEARS, BO RHAP, LIVE AID, THE FULL AMAZING STORY
PLUS THEIR 50 GREATEST SONGS - VOTED FOR BY YOU

UNOFFICIAL

> Chart the rise of Queen, from their early years to international stardom

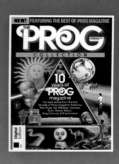

NEW! FEATURING THE BEST OF PROG MAGAZINE

THE **PROG** COLLECTION

10 years of PROG magazine

Digital Edition

Rock

LED ZEPPELIN

Digital Edition

Guitarist GUIDE TO

Effects PEDALS

GENESIS

THE COMPLETE STORY!

Digital Edition

100% UNOFFICIAL

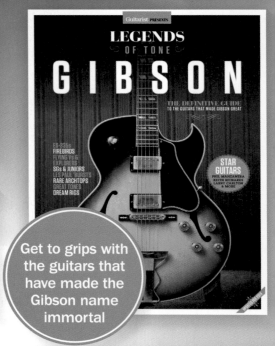

Guitarist PRESENTS

LEGENDS OF TONE

GIBSON

THE DEFINITIVE GUIDE
TO THE GUITARS THAT MADE GIBSON GREAT

ES-335s
FIREBIRDS
FLYING Vs &
EXPLORERS
SGs & JUNIORS
LES PAUL 'BURSTS'
RARE ARCHTOPS
GREAT TONES
DREAM RIGS

STAR GUITARS
PHIL MANZANERA
KEITH RICHARDS
LARRY CARLTON
& MORE

THE STORY OF THE
BEATLES
The complete guide to the greatest band of all time

Digital Edition

The Fab Four • Discography • Beatlemania • Behind the scenes

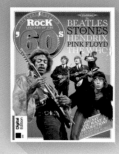

Rock
'60s

BEATLES
STONES
HENDRIX
PINK FLOYD
THE WHO

Digital Edition

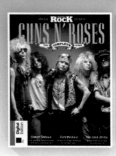

Rock EDITION

GUNS N' ROSES

THE COMPLETE GUIDE

Digital Edition

> Get to grips with the guitars that have made the Gibson name immortal

The Story of
The **Rolling Stones** 55

Digital Edition

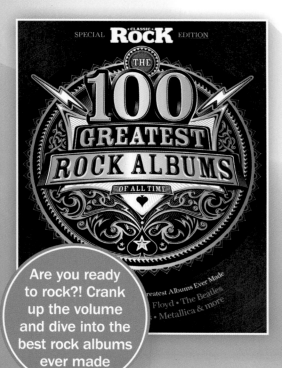

SPECIAL **CLASSIC Rock** EDITION

THE
100 GREATEST ROCK ALBUMS
OF ALL TIME

Greatest Albums Ever Made
...Floyd • The Beatles
...Metallica & more

> Are you ready to rock?! Crank up the volume and dive into the best rock albums ever made

SLIPKNOT
THE COMPLETE STORY

EXCLUSIVE INTERVIEWS
THE STORY BEHIND EVERY ALBUM
AT HOME WITH COREY TAYLOR

Digital Edition

PLAY LIKE YOUR HEROES!
THE ULTIMATE COLLECTION

Blues

LEGENDARY TABBED LICKS

HUBERT SUMLIN

Digital Edition

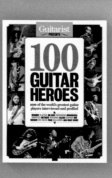

Guitarist PRESENTS

100 GUITAR HEROES

100 of the world's greatest guitar players interviewed and profiled

Guitarist PRESENTS
BUY & PLAY

The Acoustic Guitar

REVISED & UPDATED FOR 2018

NEW! MUSIC MILESTONES

PINK FLOYD
ALBUM BY ALBUM: THE DEFINITIVE HISTORY

Digital Edition

Get great savings when you buy direct from us

1000s of great titles, many not available anywhere else

World-wide delivery and super-safe ordering

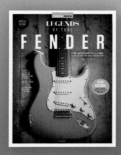

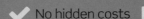 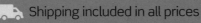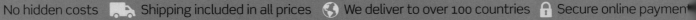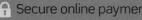